No Man's Stage
A Semiotic Study of
Jean Genet's Major Plays

Theater and Dramatic Studies, No. 34

Oscar G. Brockett, Series Editor

Leslie Waggener Professor of Fine Arts
and Professor of Drama
The University of Texas at Austin

Bernard Beckerman, Series Editor, 1980-1983

Brander Matthews Professor of Dramatic Literature
Columbia University in the City of New York

Other Titles in This Series

No Man's Stage
A Semiotic Study of
Jean Genet's Major Plays

by
Una Chaudhuri

UMI RESEARCH PRESS
Ann Arbor, Michigan

Produced and distributed by
UMI Research Press
an imprint of
University Microfilms, Inc.
Ann Arbor, Michigan 48106

Library of Congress Cataloging in Publication Data

Chaudhuri, Una, 1951-
   No man's stage.

   (Studies in modern literature ; no. 34)
   Revisions of thesis (Ph.D)—Columbia University,
1982.
   Bibliography: p.
   Includes index.
   1. Genet, Jean, 1910-   —Criticism and
interpretation.   2. Semiotics and literature.
I. Title.   II. Series.
PQ2613.E53Z5825   1986   842'.912   85-28886
ISBN 0-8357-1731-3 (alk. paper)

For Michael Vannoy Adams

Contents

Acknowledgments

I wish to thank Grove Press and Rosica Colin Ltd. for permission to quote from the plays of Jean Genet, and the editors of *Modern Drama* for permission to reprint parts of an article on *The Blacks* that appeared in the September 1985 issue of that journal.

Of the many teachers, colleagues and friends who have helped and encouraged me over the years, I wish especially to acknowledge Professors Michael Hays, Olga Ragusi and Michael Riffaterre of Columbia University, who read this work during its early stages and made many valuable contributions to it. Professor Martin Meisel not only read and helped to shape this study at that early stage, but remained closely involved with it through its transformation into a book. I deeply appreciate his kindness and support. I must also thank my teachers at Delhi University, especially Professor Rupin Desai, who first introduced me to the pleasures of the text, and my dear friends Adhip Chaudhuri, Amit Shah and Gauri Viswanathan, who shared those and other pleasures, then and since. Their unfailing love and support have helped me to make a place for myself not only in a demanding profession but also in a new country.

My greatest debt for this book is to Professor Bernard Beckerman of Columbia University; my greatest regret, that I will not be able to share its completion with him. His recent death meant the loss not only of one of the most distinguished scholars in the field of drama but also of a friend, whose wisdom, warmth and concern were such as to turn writing into an intellectual and personal adventure. For what Professor Beckerman taught me about drama, and for how he taught it, I am deeply grateful.

Two people remained to be thanked. The first is my husband, Michael Vannoy Adams, whose commitment to ideas has been and remains my greatest inspiration, and who has contributed far more to this book and to my intellectual life than a mere dedication can repay. The second is my mother, Usha Baljit Singh, whose example and encouragement have meant more to me than I can express.

1

Introduction

But I would rather say a few words about the theatre in general.
I dislike it.

Jean Genet, "A Note on Theatre"

The hermeneutic problem posed by the drama of Jean Genet, a problem which
has resulted in the various and contradictory classifications of his works as
realistic, absurdist, revolutionary, conservative, modernist, classical,
political, anarchist, psychological, ritualistic, Brechtian, Artaudian, and so
on, is only partially contingent upon the writer's notorious perversity, a
perversity manifested in the relentless pursuit of the objects, including theater,
of his own disgust. While this perversity does, as we shall see, exercise an
irresistible attraction for critics, converting even the most rigorously aesthetic
approaches into ultimately moralistic ones, the real source of the problem lies
in the dynamic of negation itself, and its apparently inevitable development
into some positive system. Denial, whether manifested on the ethical plane as
immorality, or on the aesthetic plane as disunity, seems unable to resist
transformation, through sustained logical analysis, into some stable
affirmation. Once systematized, negation is also neutralized—denatured—
and the possibility of capturing it, either in criticism or in performance,
already outstripped.

The hermeneutic problem is compounded in the case of a living writer
who, dedicated to destruction but seduced by system, acquiesces in one such
interpretation, approves and validates it, and begins to represent himself and
his work through it. Thus it is with Jean Genet and the "saintly" system
constructed for him by his friend Jean-Paul Sartre. While a work of the
mammoth proportions and impressive authorship of *Saint Genet: Actor and
Martyr* requires little in the way of outside support to establish itself, overt
and express approval by its subject has the effect of establishing it in a position
of unshakable interpretive power and critical authority. Although written
before the appearance of Genet's major plays, Sartre's study, stamped with

Genet's approval, exerts its influence on all succeeding scholarship. Indeed, it would hardly be an exaggeration to say that Genet criticism, at least until recently,[1] was both initiated and exhausted in Sartre's extraordinary existential psychobiography. This literary curiosity, a monumental study of an unknown criminal and writer by a leading philosopher of the age, has had the effect of creating, in its turn, a literary freak: a petrified legend who is still a living, changing, experimenting writer, a psychosocial model who is also a unique individual, a "being," as Richard Coe says, "known for reference as Jean Genet."[2] It is this semifictional subject, as much as the objects of his creation, who, all too often, is discovered, explained, analyzed, and rediscovered in Genet criticism.

The wide prevalence of this critical phenomenon is hardly surprising. Sartre's Genet, poised forever between self-consciousness and personal alienation, self and other, perceiver and object of perception, is not only a symbolic construct of great power and fascination, but also a stable and unified system of reconciled contradictions, the perfect solution to the moral and aesthetic dilemmas which plagued his early critics. That this legend should structure so many studies of Genet's work is hardly surprising, but it is, nonetheless, unfortunate. For its restrictive, even blinding effect on criticism is undeniable.

It creates, first of all, a continuity in criticism which all but disregards the implications of Genet's change of medium, his shift from novelist to playwright. In the few cases where this question is addressed, it serves simply to bolster a biographical approach to Genet's works, the second major effect of Sartre's study. Genet's movement from page to stage is seen simply as a felicitous functional development, the discovery of a form better suited than the novel to his obsessive themes.

Thus, Claude Bonnefoy, in a thematic study of Genet's work which deals with the novels and plays simultaneously, presents Genet's movement into drama as further evidence of the obsessive quality of Genet's creativity, its capacity to wrench all subjects and forms into one single and personal purpose. Although Genet's "mythology is not fixed," says Bonnefoy, and "does not exclude the appearance of new themes or a modification of the vision," in Genet's work "all new experience, be it of the order of the lived or of literary technique, soon roots itself deeply in his personal universe. Rapidly, he makes it his. Thus when, twice, he happened to write a play on request, *The Maids* for Louis Jouvet and *The Blacks* for a group of black actors, the Griots, he could not do it without injecting his personal fantasies into the drama."[3]

Or, in critiques even more committed to a psychobiographical reading of the works, the plays are seen as Genet's way of realizing his alleged ideal of living-through-others, others who themselves were actualized through borrowed gestures. Thus, according to Jean-Marie Magnan, Genet the novelist "would copy an ideal hero to whom an actor of the milieu, Stilitano or some other pimp, lent life. To be Stilitano—beautiful appearance, collection of gestures already borrowed—Genet attempted to steal his gestures."[4] The writer sees *The Balcony* as a further step in this quest: "It may be that *The Balcony* has as its main objective to deliver Genet from gestures, to disenchant him."[5]

The biographical bias also affects dramatic criticism adversely in its tendency to apply, to dramatic characters and situations, psychological and philosophical categories which Sartre's analysis had shown to be appropriate and fruitful in the more autobiographical and personal context of the novels. Thus we find interpretations based on elaborate identifications between Genet and his characters. Magnan sees Genet occupying, in *The Balcony*, the same position as Irma: "he finds himself at the center with Mme Irma, and succeeds in organizing around himself this sumptuous theater: a celebration whose splendors envelop him and hide him from the world."[6] In discussing *The Screens*, the same critic employs the term "Genet-Saïd,"[7] thus positing a primarily personal, psychological action which makes of the play a means of personal liberation. Such identifications also exemplify the third and final effect of Sartre's approach: a compulsion to discover the moral roots and goals of Genet's artistic endeavor. This, the most insidious and disturbing of tendencies in Genet criticism, deserves close scrutiny.

Sartre's Genet, trapped forever in the moment of his nominal transformation from innocent child to scheming criminal, eternally reliving the rape of his unselfconscious existence by the pointed fingers of word-wielding accusers, knows himself to be sentenced to an irreversible negative definition. The title of thief cleaves to him like the enforced convict's uniform, and, like a costume, it is both a sign of himself and yet not himself. It is a role, but one that seeps into him, one without which he would be empty and invisible. Experiencing himself thus, as a surface, Genet develops a lucid schizophrenia, and seeks actively to embody this alien self which is not himself but which is nothing else. Like his Blacks, he exploits the only freedom available to him: that of rigorously pursuing this imposed and negative definition. But the pursuit, once transposed—or sublimated—into the realm of art, suffers a queer metamorphosis. It becomes not merely a personal liberation, but also an exemplary act of self-sacrifice, a personal crucifixion for the salvation of one's late detractors. By means of an "artistic alchemy"[8] Genet not only replaces a vile life with a beautiful artwork, but generalizes his pain into a collective ritual. Of the stuff of his antisocial urges and perverse fantasies he makes an altar at which we may all worship. His plays liberate both him and us; they exorcise our demons, our dark urges, our cruelty. Suddenly, this monster is our savior: generous, altruistic, and—yes—saintly.

This glowing account of Genet's enterprise achieves two things: it neutralizes his radical revolt, reversing it, turning it into a pernicious religiosity, and it manages to assign him a place in post-Artaudian theatrical history. The studies by Joseph McMahon and Richard Coe exemplify the first effect, Robert Brustein's chapter on Genet in *The Theater of Revolt* the second.[9] In all three, as in political approaches like Philip Thody's, sociological ones like Lucien Goldmann's, and mythological ones like Lewis Cetta's, Sartre's influence is strongly felt.[10] Its overall effect is that analysis proceeds at the conceptual level and attention is focused on that structural level (the verbal) which the plays share with the novels, and this in spite of Genet's insistence that "in the theater, all takes place in the visible world and nowhere else."[11]

Joseph McMahon's *The Imagination of Jean Genet,* while dissociating itself from Sartre both substantively and methodologically, nevertheless fails to escape the limitations of a fundamentally psychological framework. McMahon criticizes the "sentimentalism" which ascribes, as Sartre does, all of Genet's disturbing celebrations of evil and criminality to the repressive action of a heterosexual and propertied bourgeois society; he offers instead an interpretation that places more emphasis on the individual's own, inherent, instinctual brand of pleasure and desire. But the chronicle he presents of the expression of this desire becomes eventually an answer to a moral question: how does the criminal turn artist, win society over to his side, and gain an audience? How is he able to neutralize—even temporarily—those he seeks to revile? The question had already been raised in France, and answered negatively by Georges Bataille, who concluded that Genet had neither the desire nor the power to communicate his perverted perceptions and preoccupations to others. Defining true literary communication as something transcending the individual author and reader, "a sovereign author addresses sovereign humanity, beyond the servitude of the isolated reader",[12] an act in which "the author denies himself," Bataille finds Genet failing to achieve such communication by virtue of a refusal to deny "his own peculiarities in favor of the work."[13] Far from transcending himself in his work (as many critics suggest), Genet is, Bataille insists, trapped, *personally* trapped, in it. His work "is the fretting of a crotchety individual," mesmerized by his weaknesses, his limitations, his "profound *servitude*" (emphasis in original)[14]—the very things that must be denied in order to achieve the "sovereignty" of true literary communication.

McMahon, however, sees the desire to communicate as the central motivation of Genet's artistic career; indeed, Genet's development appears to McMahon as nothing less than an odyssey of personal liberation, wherein artistic achievement represents a triumph over the individual's moral and psychological insufficiencies. The *power* to communicate is also present, but it is dependent on a kind of subterfuge, a trick. Distinguishing between the "instinctive" (perverse) and "representational" (poetic) parts of Genet's imagination, McMahon sees him successfully enlisting the latter in a rape of the audience's aesthetic sensibilities, seducing it into a participation—albeit a temporary and fleeting one—in the former.

To anyone who has felt the almost palpable sensuality of Genet's prose, his extravagant, luxuriant webs of sonorous words and phrases, McMahon's account does ring true. Upon closer examination, however, it reveals several problems, and even seems to harbor some unresolved contradictions. The most disturbing of these is the critic's easy assimilation, into the same process, of both shock and seduction, repulsion and attraction. The coincidence of these contradictory affective operations is explained by McMahon by means of a complicated (and strongly moralistic) psychological proposition: a hypocritical audience, unknowing victims of an easily eroded double standard. Genet deceives, and succeeds in his deception, because the shocking images he presents are precisely those most cherished by his audience, those lurking in secret consensus beneath a false surface of established and coherent morality. As deceiver, as forger of audience sympathies for ultimately untenable positions, Genet is compared to Sophocles—a Sophocles minus his complicitous audience, or rather a Sophocles forced to reveal the hidden and shameful complicity of his audience through shock and seduction. In this aggressive unveiling of the audience to itself, this violent piercing of a defunct morality, Genet emerges as the committed moralist, holding the mirror up to us that we may finally face our degradation. The conclusion returns McMahon to the biographical and morally evaluative focus he had so emphatically repudiated at the outset, demonstrating the tendency, mentioned earlier, of even the most consciously aesthetic approaches to devolve finally into moral essays.

Richard Coe, in *The Vision of Jean Genet,* provides possibly the finest example of a philosophical reading of Genet's works. Once again, as Coe describes Genet in terms of a dialectic of the two halves of a split consciousness, a psychological version of the Being and Nothingness opposition, Sartre's presence is strongly felt. To Coe, Genet is the "poet of solitude," creating poetry out of conflict, unity out of contradiction, by the fabrication of a third, "visionary" consciousness, a reflection of the two initial reflections of the divided self. This is art as apotheosis, a distanced, disengaged, "elevated" perspective from which the poet and his audience contemplate an otherwise painful, dangerous, and destructive schizophrenic consciousness.

McMahon and Coe are superior representatives of the predominant trend in Genet criticism; their starting point is biography, their method thematic, their conclusions abstract and philosophical. Basically, they explicate the verbal fabric of Genet's plays, seeing conceptual systems which merely reiterate, in disguise, Sartre's existential analysis.

My first objection to this critical trend is methodological: it all but ignores the specifically theatrical elements of the plays, and concentrates too exclusively on their literary elements. My second and more important objection is to the conclusion it draws, a conclusion which reveals its inadequacy when viewed in the context of *dramatic* theory.

The critical verdict that emerges from philosophically oriented approaches to Genet is that his dramatic practice is original, provocative, brilliant, but finally doomed. Dedicated to nothingness and its moral correlative, evil, Genet is seen to slip quickly into a metaphysical whirligig of illusion and reality, subject and object, mind and matter, until his message finally freezes into a static and impotent image: consciousness as the mutual reflection of two empty mirrors, endlessly reflecting each other's reflections. Genet's ubiquitous "mirror symbol" and all its metaphysical implications have been fully elucidated and need no further rehearsal (but much remains to be understood about the inclusion, in the signifying stage space, of such flagrantly illusory, duplicated and framed moving images as mirrors provide). The mirror as theme or symbol, however (like the subject of evil, whose pursuit and vigorous espousal have won Genet his existential sainthood), is surely exhausted. The philosophical approach brings Genet criticism to a shaky conclusion: having denied all positives—historical, social, political and personal—Genet must, in a final twist, deny negation itself and make of appearance, of form, the final reality and truth. In a display of logic matched in self-destructiveness only by Milton's Satan, Genet ruins his revolutions, restores his brothels of pretense to real authority, revives his murdered white aristocrats, and denies the possibility of a benign conclusion even in death. In pursuing this logic he exhausts its limits, ending, not even where he began, but nowhere, in a fog of ambiguity. He is, finally, not the poet of evil, or of solitude, or even of nothingness, but the poet of impossibility.

The notion of an impossible theater, a doomed artistic enterprise seeking to unify its vision of a fragmented and ruptured world, to give ritualistic plenitude and coherence to an experience of isolation and impoverishment, is an intuitively acceptable but theoretically unstable account of much modern drama, including Genet's. From a strictly theoretical point of view, it raises more questions than it answers. For how can nothingness, and its processive antecedent, negation, be evoked and implemented in the intensely physical medium that is the theater? How can an art form so mired in matter, so steeped in substance, be used to express nonbeing? How can a context so inherently restricted to the here and now, to the present and to presence, be used to convey instead the nowhere and the never, total absence? Genet is not the only modern playwright of whom it can be asked whether his denial is destined to remain at the verbal and conceptual level, at every moment contradicted by his stage, or whether he has found a way, as Artaud demanded, to "deny in the concrete."

These questions take one to the very heart of the theater, to that definitional core which, in recent decades, has furnished "theatricalist" playwrights with a fruitful theme. It takes one also to the theories of Antonin Artaud, or rather to the Artaudian problematic of which theatrical "impossibility" is the logical outcome.

Metatheater: Theory and Practice

The paradoxes of a theatrical vision which insists on denial as its central assertion had begun to be rehearsed decades before they received their first full-dress presentation in the writings of Antonin Artaud. On stages still resounding with that much rolled and relished miracle of public provocation with which Père Ubu had greeted his first audience, the initial paradox, a dramatic construct designed for and committed to destruction, had been proliferating, multiplying contradictions. The original contradiction, evident already as Ubu was rapidly transformed from an object of outrage into one of amusement, even approval, the contradiction inherent in all radical theatrical provocation, which requires the attention, if not the approval, of the very consciousness it seeks to challenge and destroy, this original contradiction was destined to form but the cornerstone of an elaborate edifice of paradoxes. Apparently doomed from the outset to struggle against its own definition, the avant-garde responded by integrating its problematic, incorporating upon its stages the multiple oppositions it had experienced in confronting audiences.

By 1930, every description and definition of avant-garde theater must accept a rhetoric of contradiction. The new tradition is revolution, the new ideal, physicality, the new reality, dream, the new order, anarchy. Experimentation itself, the quest for difference and novelty, attains such proportions as to risk metamorphosis into a mainstream, an establishment. Thus when, after Ubu, after Dada, after Surrealism, Futurism, Constructivism, Orphism, Vorticism, Primitivism, Theatricalism, after all the frenzied "concrete denials" of the *entre-guerres* years, Artaud's *The Theater and Its Double* makes its appearance, it does so on the horizon of an already radicalized theatrical consciousness. It comes as a culmination, but proves its ancestry by eschewing any stable logicality, by denying itself the luxury of closure. The Theater of Cruelty appears, and remains invisible. If Antonin Artaud (along with others) represents major trends characteristic of twentieth-century theatrical consciousness, he does so not by virtue of his substantive displacement of the social and psychological in favor of the primitive and primeval, nor by virtue of his philosophical substitution of a transcendent vision for the positivistic metaphysics upon which the mimetic tradition of Occidental theater had rested, nor even by virtue of his practical transference of theatrical semiosis from the literary-conceptual to the material-experiential realm, but rather by virtue of his theoretical rendition, final and comprehensive, of an impossible theater. Like the theater he demands, Artaud himself embodies paradox. Espousing exile and marginality, he becomes a central theoretical force. Conceptualizing the material life of the theater, he inscribes a vision, visualizes the unseen, affirms negation, asserts denial, and insists upon impossibility.

The stage survives these contradictions. Indeed, it thrives on them. They enliven it, creating endless versions of the theatrical dynamic, providing practitioners and spectators with continually renewed possibilities for unique interactions. Upon the denial of traditional aesthetic norms is predicated a new and fluid hierarchy of theatrical elements, whereby temporary ascendancy is enjoyed in turn by director, actor, designer, even spectator. Often, now, the burden of signification, lifted from the playwright and his linguistic text, divides itself more equitably between various theatrical elements and entities, creating not only new techniques and effects, but also new subjects. Of the latter, perhaps the most fertile turns out to be the stage itself, the stage as object of aesthetic experimentation and philosophical contemplation, the so-called "self-conscious stage" of modern drama. Duplicating the reflexive mode characteristic of modernism in general, the theater embarks upon a spirited self-analysis.

Of the many directions theatrical reflexivity takes, and the many areas into which these lead, several resemble traditional dramatic concerns enough to allow a continuity in the critical tradition. For, if stage practice flourished in paradox and contradiction, critical theory had been radically threatened by it. Relying on language, drama criticism has always been a literary activity, most at home with verbal signification, most receptive to literary semiosis. For such an orientation, the postverbal stage remains opaque, a material maze through which the old words wander unconvincingly, without arrivals, an airy fortress to which the traditional critical categories lay siege in vain. Familiar analytic procedures, such as the discovery of meaning in plot structures, the psychological analysis of dramatic characters, the elucidation of themes and their constitutive symbols, the evaluation of a writer's philosophical insights and messages—all predicated upon a dramaturgy of absence, of mimesis, of representation—rebound uselessly when applied to a theater which refers primarily to itself, presenting (instead of representing) an actor and a stage liberated from their functions as signifiers of an absent, prior, and privileged significance.

However, while the acute, insistent theatricality of much modern drama challenges traditional criticism, this very reflexivity can also rescue it from this impasse. The "self-conscious stage" has the curious effect of allowing itself—the stage *qua* stage—to function as a sign of, or to *appear* to symbolize, other realms of reality.

Before long, the old Shakespearean metatheatrical formula—"all the world's a stage"—is variously resurrected, and subjected to exhaustive analysis and comprehensive explication. "Pirandellism," of which Pirandello's works constitute only the core, provides critics with untold opportunities to rehearse the philosophical, sociological, and psychological implications of the great theatrical themes of illusion, pretense, and appearance. From play-acting to role-playing, from stage to life, whole volumes are devoted to subtle descriptions of man the actor. Over and over again, with critical apparatuses borrowed from psychology, anthropology, political science, we are shown the spectacle of his desperate posturings on the various "stages" of human life—in his relationships, in politics, in his own fragmented consciousness.[15]

While often brilliantly done, these analyses remain literary and abstract, quickly translating theatricalist phenomena (such as characters who are actors, brothels which are playhouses,and a stage which represents a stage) into thematic terms: Genet's interest is seen to lie not in theater *per se*, but in the analogies it furnishes to certain psychological and social phenomena (such as role-playing, reliance on appearances, instability of experience, inauthenticity, etc.). Thus, according to Edith Melcher, Genet uses the theater as Pirandello did, to dramatize a conflict between the flux of life and the permanence of art. In this conflict, art, or rather fiction, emerges as the victor, having the advantage of coherence and control, which life lacks. Art becomes reality, fiction becomes truth, and "the only absolute truth is that there is none, nothing is certain in human experience until it achieves the permanence of art, that is of death."[16] This conclusion is not only theoretically unsatisfactory (for instance, it fails to explain how the "reality" that is to be undermined exists in the play, which is, after all, a fictional construct); it is also contradicted by the tremendous instability and lack of clear, final statement in Genet's plays.

Stanley Eskin relates the theme to Sartre's account of Genet's psychology, and sees Genet as a militant psychosocial critic satirizing the culture's deep-seated sexual malaise, exposing the deadly alliance it has forged between masquerade, death, and pleasure. Since Genet's vision proceeds not from detached observation but from the guilty participation of the professional homosexual, it functions not as a liberating recognition but a hopeless confession, a final acknowledgment of, and acquiescence in, his degraded condition. Eskin denies Genet even the possibility of an "artistic" consolation like Pirandello's. This is the impotency of the utterly subjugated negativist: "All the other avant-garde playwrights—Ionesco, Beckett, Adamov, Golser, and before them Cocteau, Pirandello, Jarry have a center of vitality against which are measured their pessimism, their bleakness, their sense of irony, futility, or incongruity. But not Genet: his work, firmly anchored in sterility and death, struggles ponderously to create dramatic tension between nothingness and more nothingness. *In this he does not succeed*" (my emphasis).[17] Here, again, is the "impossibilist" Genet, or Genet the victim of impossibility. Finally, even Lionel Abel, the originator of the term "metatheater," reaches the same conclusion about Genet's reflexive dramaturgy: "having absorbed the revolution with its insistence on reality into the illusionist world of The Great Balcony, Genet suddenly reverses himself and tries to see illusion itself as inexorable. But *this is an impossible idea, contrary to dramatic judgment or good sense...*" (my emphasis).[18]

Long ago, Sartre had talked about "the ontological failure" of evil, which constantly "pursues its own nothingness." The idea, as we have seen, leads inevitably to a pitying evaluation of Genet's enterprise. It is not my intention to argue against this verdict, at least not in the realm of philosophical criticism where past analysis has been conducted. Indeed, the idea that Genet's philosophical position is illogical and untenable is, in itself, quite acceptable, and even probable. My objections are methodological: I feel that the idea has been erroneously derived, and that it raises questions of dramatic theory which must be answered before this interpretation can be accepted. I propose a different genre of analysis, one which would focus on the specifically theatrical, performative elements of Genet's drama, according them appropriate significative status in the communicative structure. I believe that it is only on the basis of some such analysis, which would examine Genet's handling of such theatrical constants as stage space and performance time, movement and gesture, staging and setting, light and color, sound and speech, that his thematic concerns might be enunciated. It is within this area also that I would like to pose the question of Impossibility as well, and document the theatrical techniques of negation.

Such a proposal is a response, in fact, to an endemic critical problem, one forced into the open by the avant-garde practice described above. As mentioned earlier, traditional drama theory has responded primarily to the linguistic component of theater, this emphasis then leading it to develop the response within a conceptual framework borrowed from literary discourse. Much contemporary theater, with its attention to the concrete and present elements of theater, of which language is only one, serves to dramatize the need for a critical discourse capable of accounting for all of theater, instead of rendering it approximate, or analogous, to literature. It requires the development of a critical method which recognizes the expressive and communicative potential of concrete elements, their autonomous functioning as signs in a special system of signification, instead of as mere illustrations of ideas located in a verbal fabric which exists before and behind its physical manifestation. Without such a method, criticism of the avant-garde can be no more than what we have seen: an imprecise, quasi-philosophical, and impotent recognition of impossibility.

The semiotics of theater (by which I mean the development of the theory of signs in the area of drama and theater, not the actual sign usage of plays, which I will call *semiosis*) differs from traditional drama criticism in two important ways. The first is that it constitutes its subject of study (theater) differently: it defines the theater as a *polysystem*, that is, a signifying system made up of the combination and interplay of several distinct systems, of which language is (only) one. While it recognizes the primacy of language in *certain* dramatic codes (or types), it does not automatically or tacitly assume this to be the case with all drama, as traditional drama criticism does. Secondly, and most crucially, it pursues the task of *description* rather than *interpretation* vis-à-vis dramatic texts: it studies *meaning-production* rather than *meaning*. In this orientation it resembles avant-garde theater itself, which has also been called "the theater of research."[19] The resemblance is by no means accidental: the rise of theater semiotics shares a historical moment—and hence a conceptual orientation—with avant-garde theater. It has thus constituted itself largely in ways that avoid the pitfalls which were responsible for the failure of traditional criticism vis-à-vis avant-garde theater (the most significant such pitfall being that of privileging language, which semiotics avoids by means of the "polysystem" foundation mentioned above).

However, the interpretive tradition is not easily shaken off. It insinuates itself into semiotic study, sometimes to such an extent that nonverbal signs are discussed mainly as vehicles or symbols of previously identified "themes." For example, the familiar Sartrian psychobiographical premise surfaces again in a recent study of concrete elements (objects and space) in *The Balcony*. Sartre's suggestion that Genet experienced a kind of death when he was chased from his childhood paradise by being declared a thief becomes the premise from which this critic, Y. Went-Daoust, sees the mirrors of the play, for instance, as "indispensable auxiliaries in the search for appearance,"[20] a search which leads to "a definitive fixity, the ideal fixity of death."[21] Other objects and places are also seen as symbols for the theme established by Sartre and elaborated by later critics. Organizing all the concrete elements of the play along a familiar opposition—illusion (positive) versus reality (negative)—the analysis presents a static and reductive account of the play. The photographers, to cite just one example, are seen (by virtue of their location within the house of illusions) as a privileged and positive force, equal in image-making power to the mirrors, the loci of the "pure reflection." "The Photographers form a group privileged by their very profession. On a level with the mirrors, they rival them in the effort to realize the image."[22] This analysis is in flagrant contradiction to Genet's very negative and mechanical characterization of the photographers, who terrorize and manipulate their subjects, using their cameras like guns. The images they achieve are cynical and fraudulent, totally implicated in the circuit of power which the Figures seek to escape.

An interpretive bias also governs the decision of another study[23] to treat all "categories" of objects simultaneously and without distinction, although carefully distinguishing them at the outset as follows: (1) objects shown, (2) objects shown and named, and (3) objects named: "The importance of the text being very great in Genet, it seems logical to accord as much importance to one category as to another and to consider that all three are constitutive of the same represented universe."[24] From a semiotic point of view, this is clearly an unwarranted decision; the "stuff" of various signs (the material of their signifiers) is of great importance: to ignore it is to imply a linguistic model for everything in the theater, including nonlinguistic signs. It is to import the word-thing equation of mimetic language into the realm of objects, which are then seen as material "words" standing for objects equally well referred to with words. Thus the ensuing analysis, while it furnishes a thorough tabulation of all mentions (verbal or physical) of various objects, is dedicated to spelling out *what* all these objects say, rather than *how,* in the theatrical context, they say it. The main "objects" discussed are: mirrors, lace, water, and blood, and the main semantic field they are seen to occupy is that organized by the opposition movement (= flow, liquid, life, reality) vs. fixity (= coagulation, death, illusion). The study, which lists all instances of object reference in the play, treats these objects as literary symbols rather than theatrical signs. In doing so, it undoubtedly reveals some of the motifs which, at a microlevel, contribute to the play's larger themes, but it does not really take the actual *theatrical* use of these objects into account.

By contrast, Michèle Piemme's analysis of "Scenic Space and Dramatic Illusion in *The Balcony*" is exemplary of semiotic description.[25] Piemme, remaining close to the actual stage practice required by the play, provides a lucid explanation of the way the play functions, concluding: "The play is not 'a satire of this or that', which would merely situate its power at the level of content. It denounces at the same time its own means of production as well as the product it engenders. It is a satire, intrinsically, even at the level of signifiers."[26]

Here, finally, is a concretely grounded discussion of what has for so long been vaguely discussed as "metatheater." The virtue of Piemme's analysis is that it never ceases to follow the flow of signs from stage to spectator, never loses sight of the experience of *watching* the play (instead of trying simply to elucidate its [postperformance] "meaning").

Piemme's recognition of the primacy of theatrical *experience* and signifying *method* in the "message" of Genet's drama is shared by another study, Jean Gitenet's "Profane and Sacred Reality in Jean Genet's Theater."[27] Though so brief as to be almost aphoristic, Gitenet's piece precisely identifies a central strategy of Genet's drama: the assertion of a certain order of reality by an overrealization of its opposite: a process of *simultaneous* affirmation and negation of two mutually opposing realms. "Consequently, we believe that Genet's theater is not a presentation of the sacred world, a kind of discovery of a presupposed universe, contrary to the profane world; it is truly a *sacralization* (the sacred in action)" (emphasis in original).[28]

Piemme's and Gitenet's studies are, in my view, examples of the kind of new, nonthematic focus that can take avant-garde criticism beyond the old verdict of impossibility. In the study of Genet's plays that I propose this new focus is crucial. It is Genet's concrete theatrical strategies I wish to research and describe, for I believe that only on the basis of an understanding of these will the significance of his plays emerge.

2

The Semiotics of Theater

The problems of semiotic theory bear a strong family resemblance to those I have identified in avant-garde theater practice, for both activities share the difficult epistemological condition of reflexivity. The avant-garde theater strives to enact or perform theatricality and performance itself, and semiotics attempts to signify about signification as such. Both rapidly arrive at the borders of impossibility, where critical activity is transformed into self-critical theory: "Semiotics cannot develop except as a critique of semiotics.... Research in semiotics remains an investigation which discovers nothing at the end of its quest but its own ideological mores, so as to take cognizance of them, to deny them, and to start out anew."[1] The resemblance need not stop here, however, for semiotics may also share with theater the more positive interim activity of original analysis, of uncovering hitherto hidden facets of its object of study.

It has sometimes been objected that this capacity of semiotics has not been revealed to any great extent as yet, as evidenced by the relative paucity of original semiotic analyses of dramatic texts. This objection may in part be born of a deep misconception about semiotics and its tasks, specifically, the erroneous notion that semiotics, like other literary methods, seeks primarily to produce new and better interpretations of texts. In actual fact, the focus of semiotic study need not be the text at all (although the study of texts is not, by any means, outside the domain of semiotic analysis). Even if theater semiotics had not yet begun to study whole dramatic texts (which, however, it has, and with great success),[2] and even if it were still pursuing the kind of inquiry into the smallest and most concrete aspects of theatrical signification which distinguished its early stages,[3] there would be no cause for alarm. The decision to restrict oneself, at the outset, to a scrutiny of the most concrete phenomena is, as Umberto Eco has pointed out, essential and wise.[4] It is analogous to the restriction the founders of modern linguistics imposed on themselves when they chose to deal first with phonemes and words instead of leaping ahead to a study of sentences and texts. The temptation to work with abstract and general questions is a strong one, and should be avoided even at the cost of having impatient colleagues conclude that the theory is critically impotent. In this respect, Eco's analogy with architecture is compelling: "I fought strenuously against certain semioticians of architecture who maintained that Palladio's villas are architecture while public urinals, log cabins and dog's beds are not—refusing to understand that if there is a 'language' of architecture it basically arose when the first man nailed a stick in the ground to shape a space (the space around the stick vs. the space far from the stick). . . . "[5] The foundations of theater semiotics were laid by those who assumed the "naive attitude" towards the subject that Eco demands, and held at bay the more traditional questions of the abstract meanings of a total dramatic text. This strategy is bound to arouse—and has—much impatience from the "spectators" of this theoretical performance, but it is an impatience born of false expectations and consequently one that will dissipate as those expectations are gradually altered.

The issue is ultimately a pragmatic one: what are texts *for?* They have for some time now[6] been assumed (by practitioners of a wide range of methods and theories) to exist as vehicles for a single, stable meaning, the discovery of which is the reader's (critic's) task. The tacit assumption of one who performs this task is that, to perform it successfully, he must identify and articulate a unified, coherent, and recognizable meaning: every operation he performs must be a step towards this goal, a contribution to this meaning. This notion, which is in fact an ideological stance characteristic of what Jacques Derrida has identified as the Western "metaphysics of presence," directs even the most rigorously stylistic and formalistic of methods. Even structuralism, which claims to restrict its inquiry to those underlying, abstract attributes of a system that allow that system to be used to convey "messages," does not escape its dictates: "When one speaks of the structure of a literary work, one does so from a certain vantage point: *one starts with notions of the meaning or effects of a poem* and tries to identify the structures responsible for those effects. Possible configurations or patterns which make no contribution are rejected as irrelevant" (my emphasis).[7]

In recent years, some literary theory—especially of the Deconstructionist school associated with Derrida and the Tel Quel group—has attempted to challenge this critical paradigm, to displace the "center"—that prepostulated meaning or effect—during analysis. Such an attempt strikes at the heart of traditional critical theory with its "commitment to interpretation as the proper activity of criticism."[8] Not surprisingly, therefore, this move to take critical practice "beyond interpretation"[9] has often encountered an outraged, scandalized opposition.

The semiotic analysis of dramatic texts is bound to be similarly opposed, for it will, of necessity, disappoint traditional expectations about what is or is not meaningful to say about a text. For example, semiotic analysis will frequently focus on minute aspects of a play-text, more to discover the conventions that make possible the use of that aspect as a signifying entity (a sign) than to feed into some statement of the overall meaning of the text. (For example, I will later have several pages of comments on the chandelier in *The Balcony*, most of which have little to do with any "theme" I may wish to elucidate in the play.) To fault an analysis for this may simply be to succumb to a nostalgia for uncoded, unmediated, "pure" meaning, or to manifest a prejudice against attention to the "how" as opposed to the "what" of meaning.

Semiotics imposes, as all theories do, a special kind of conceptual grid on a variety of human phenomena, an operation which, while excluding a variety of hermeneutic concerns (such as the role of natural, individual, unconscious, or obsessional factors in communication), throws into relief a set of other— conventional and collective—factors, upon which the transference of meaning depends, factors which constitute the very channels of signification and understanding available in various contexts to various communicating entities (speakers and listeners, writers and readers, painters and viewers, performers and spectators). The study it undertakes of such factors—known as "systems of signification" or "codes"[10]—reveals several normally transparent, unobserved qualities of a "message," and hence promotes a fuller understanding of the total communication.

However, new revelations about or fuller understanding of the *message* should *not* be considered the raison d'être of semiotics: such an orientation represents an interpretive bias and leads semiotics to assimilate itself (in an effort to justify its existence) to the critical tradition from which it began by distinguishing itself. The temptation to promote semiotics by using it to produce "new" or "better" readings of a text than those hitherto attained by traditional critical methods is ever-present. It has affected much semiotic analysis to date, moving the semiotician away from his sober task of describing semiosis and towards the more glamorous (and sanctioned) activity of providing new interpretations of a text. While the two procedures can sometimes coexist (especially in the case of new texts which have not yet acquired a critical tradition), the interpretive activity should be kept in careful check. The fact of the matter is that the discovery of "new" meanings in a text is precisely the opposite of the logical enterprise of semiotics, which is to *account for* the various readings a text has generated. Since semiotics is a study of the rules of signification, of the ways in which meanings are conveyed and received, it follows that previous interpretations of a text are part of its *data*, not *alternatives* to it.

This is not to say, of course, that semiotics never furnishes interpretations. It does, but typically in the case of texts containing what I will call a "semiosic theme," i.e., texts that are partly about signification, or about themselves (as signifying structures). Such texts are by no means restricted to the modern age: one of the secondary effects of semiotic orientation in recent critical thought has been the recognition of semiosic concerns in texts from other times.

The distinction between semiotic description and semiotic interpretation is crucial to the present study, which began by raising objections to the general critical verdict on Genet's drama. Such objections, it would seem, subvert or sidestep the task of semiotics, which includes paying attention to the responses a work elicits from its audience. In the case of Genet criticism, however, what we are dealing with are not the responses of the message's[11] intended receivers (spectators) but those of receivers (critics) employing a specific (and, as I believe, inappropriate) method of receiving (decoding) the messages in question. It is to this *method* that I raise objections (and my objections are of a historical nature: semiotics follows traditional drama criticism in time and so is forced into a polemic against it; in time, however, some such field as a "semiotics of drama criticism" might organize, describe, and account for the critical [as opposed to the theatrical] reception of a play, an inquiry already undertaken in the field of nondramatic literature).[12]

This study of Genet's plays is, consequently, not an attempt to discredit previous critical interpretations, but rather to employ a method of analysis that differs from theirs, one that attends to the works as sets of messages (or "global messages") framed in the *theatrical*, not the *literary*, code. Such a method, it will be seen, inevitably alters the "impossibilist" verdict described above, though it denies Genet's so-called "impossibility" only on the *theatrical*, not the philosophical, level. Spectators of these plays obtain an experience which does not square with the experience described by literary critics: it is negation, not nothingness, a process, not a product, that these plays evoke. Furthermore, especially in the case of *The Blacks*, the process of negation becomes the ground for a new affirmation, one that in no way resembles the hopeless, trapped, in-spite-of-itself affirmation traditionally attributed to Genet. This new affirmation is coded—and can only be decoded—in theatrical terms, i.e., it too is a process, not a product.

The Theatrical Code

The theater occupies a special status in semiotic theory, for it has the dubious distinction of compounding problems faced—and often overcome—in other fields of semiotic research.

Many of these problems arise out of the polysystemic nature of theater: the fact that the system of theater is actually a "system of systems" with apparently endless combinational possibilities within and between systems. Moreover, many of the so-called "systems" of theater (for example, those identified by Tadeusz Kowzan)[13] are far from being clearly distinct and mutually exclusive: "it is often less than easy to distinguish prop from set, just as 'movement', 'gesture', and 'facial mime' are in practice intimately connected and complementary aspects of the general kinesic continuum."[14] Secondly, theatrical communication is (usually) *indirect,* the messages being conveyed first between fictional senders and receivers (characters) and only then between actors and spectators. "The actor-spectator transaction within the *theatrical* context is mediated by a *dramatic* context in which a fictional speaker addresses a fictional listener."[15] This obliqueness of communication naturally confuses matters greatly, and has already given rise to a worrisome dichotomy in theater semiotics: a theoretical split between theater semiotics and drama semiotics, reflected in the title of Keir Elam's book. Indeed, the difficulties theater semiotics faces are so many and so serious that it is sometimes seen as a theoretical stillbirth, a method inherently overpowered by its object. But these difficulties can as easily be attributed to the complex nature of theater as to the inadequacies of the semiotic approach.

However, before the question of the value of the semiotic approach to theater can be answered, an even more basic question must be raised, the question of the nature—semiotic or otherwise—of theater. Is the theater a *signifying system?* Does it *communicate?* Is it a means of relaying *messages?*

The question has, at times, been answered in the negative. Georges Mounin excluded theater from the class of communication systems on the grounds that its information flow is unilateral (from performers to spectators) instead of—like language—bilateral and equal.[16] Ordinary verbal communication consists of the *full* use of a common code by both communicating entities (speakers and listeners), who can consequently change positions during the communication event—so that it becomes more proper to speak of the participants in a conversation as "interlocutors" rather than as "speakers" *or* "listeners." Clearly, this is not the case in the theater, where certain systems (such as speech, gesture, movement) are (usually) physically available only to the performers, while others (applause, laughter, etc.) usually only to the spectators. Thus, according to Mounin, the theatrical "message" is more akin to a signal or stimulus than to a sign: the latter is to be *interpreted,* the former merely *responded to.* An appropriate method of study for this phenomenon would be, therefore, not semiotics but (I suppose) cybernetics.

Besides offering an alarmingly mechanistic account of what has usually been thought of as an extremely volitional social practice, Mounin's objection also represents a misunderstanding of the nature of codes. He confuses (to use Chomsky's terms) competence and performance, or (to use Saussure's terms) *langue* and *parole.* A code can operate without requiring that everyone communicating employ it explicitly: "if the sender and the receiver know each other's code, it is not at all necessary, in order for communication to take place, that the two codes coincide, nor that they translate each other's messages exactly, nor that the two-way communication occur along the same channel."[17]

The presence, in theater, of elements analogous to all parts of the modern (Jakobsonian) communication model[18] would seem to offer an affirmative answer to our question. The play conveys *messages* in that it has a *source of emission,* a *channel of transmission,* and a *point of reception.* The first is the production group, people like the playwright, the director, the actors, the designers, the technicians, each of whom participates at different levels in the formulation of the message. The point of reception is the audience which watches the play and understands it. These latter are able to receive the messages by means of the multiple communicational channels (light waves, sound waves, etc.) available in the theater, and are able to understand it because they possess a tacit knowledge of the rules and conventions of this special social institution. Thus to the first three communication elements is added a fourth: the *code,* which is the proper study of semiotics.

However, Mounin's objection is not the only one. The theatrical code differs from other communication codes in a number of significant ways, a fact that has led some to deny that it is a code at all. Firstly, it is not purely collective and mostly stable as is, for instance, the linguistic code. The messages conveyed during a play do not simply *use* codes, they often *construct* them. This is a source of some confusion, for the practice of constructing codes is clearly rather different from that of using them: how can both practices coincide? The answer is that they do not coincide, but coexist. Since the theatrical code is a macrocode, consisting of several subcodes (e.g., the linguistic, the gestural, the kinetic, the proxemic), a given performance can employ established units of some of these subcodes while developing new versions of others. For example, much absurdist drama is distinguished by its singling out of one traditional code for revision while keeping all others constant. Ionesco's *The Chairs* recodes the furniture code, replacing its usual social (rich-poor) or aesthetic (taste-vulgarity) signifying potential with a psychological or ontological signification (presence-absence). It is in this sense that theater is both a code-abiding and code-making activity; occasionally it is even a code-breaking and code-jamming one.

Moreover, new elements of a code are introduced by individuals, a rare occurrence in the gradual historical evolution of linguistic codes. This coexistence of established, collective conventions and innovative idiosyncrasies, of publicly oriented *communication* and personally motivated *expression,* would seem, at first, to banish a good portion of the theater's functioning to a nonsemiotic realm. But once it is remembered that even the most original and personal uses of theater must perforce be theatrical, that even the most radical theatrical experimentation can be no more than the manipulation or revision of established codes, this apparent dichotomy disappears, and all operations on such codes are seen to constitute new codes, capable of sustaining a semiotic analysis.

It is worth noting that the aforementioned objection applies to all "creative" communications, and has been part of a general concern about the apparently "authoritarian" tendency of semiotics: "The concept of literary competence is a way of granting pre-eminence to certain arbitrary conventions and excluding from the realm of language all the truly creative and productive violations of these rules."[19] To regard texts *purely* as manifestations of a code is to characterize literature as a strictly, almost mechanically, rule-bound activity. Such a view is, of course, terribly repressive and dogmatic, not to mention counterintuitive. Fortunately, it is possible to think of codes in a way that allows for a more flexible, less deterministic view of the code-text relationship. "Theatrical codes," as Patrice Pavis puts it, "are 'open' codes, in perpetual evolution."[20] This evolution (the channel of which is dramatic and theatrical activity) takes the form of a development—by violation, by integration—of preexisting systems and the codes they previously supported. Thus the theater is constantly retrieving its systems from established codes, remaking them, and reorganizing them into new codes.

Secondly, the theater often seems to dispense with a code altogether. The majority of plays in the Western realistic tradition purport to represent reality itself, and their content appears (like that of a photograph)[21] as the perfect *analgon* of something that exists in the real world. Their presentation of this reality often *appears* to be uncoded: between real life and stage action there *seems* to be no reduction in size, no magnification of sound, no distortion of space, no transformation of ordinary behavioral patterns, no divergence from the norms of everyday social intercourse. This isomorphism with social reality is, of course, an illusion, or rather, a convention, a code. The transparency of the realistic code is a result not of a lack of signs but of a predominance of iconic signs, whose signifiers resemble their signifieds so closely that they are mistaken for signifieds. No matter how close the resemblance, the sign is always a sign, governed by its own system. Thus in a realistic set, every object is signified by an object without ceasing to be primarily a sign. In fact, theater, far from importing social codes wholesale, reverses the usual semiotic process: usually,[22] in life, an object (say, a chair) is first a functional object and only secondarily a sign (of poverty, taste, etc.). In the theater, a real chair is primarily a sign (the sign for "chair") and only secondarily functional.[23] The theater transforms everything, including human bodies, into signifying entities, the "words" of a theatrical language.

Far from dispensing with codes, the theater is a kind of "semiotizing machine," which transforms even "natural" signs into "artificial" ones. Even the actor, that most palpably real of objects, becomes a sign, one in which (generally) the human body is the signifier and the character the signified. In fact, the actor-sign demonstrates the extent to which the theater outstrips society in semiotic activity. So-called "natural" signs (the wrinkles on an actor's face, the pitch of his voice), which are often irrelevant to the successful operation of social codes,[24] become highly relevant in the theatrical code, for everything on stage is *chosen* by the production group. On stage the actor's natural habits and characteristics become signifiers, part of his significance; he is chosen for the role because the director considers these "natural" qualities appropriate elements of the sign he is constructing.[25] There is no play, not even the most faithful, "slice of life" naturalist play, whose very exactitude does not function as a style and communicate itself as such to the audience, guiding and controlling their response to the "reality" in question.

But if the isomorphism of theater with reality does not prevent it from being a semiotic system, it does overpower semiotic study by its resultant density and extension.[26] Since the stage often claims to represent reality, nothing real is, in principle, out of place on stage. The theater presents a whole universe of signs, signs belonging, in other social contexts, to separate semiotic systems. Thus the theatrical semiotic system appears to be a composite, heterogeneous system, made up of several homogeneous subsystems.[27] Theater semiotics, consequently, must draw on other fields of semiotics (such as linguistics, paralinguistics, kinesics, proxemics, iconology, and musicology) and, furthermore, it must study the rules governing the *interaction* of these subsystems in the theater. That this latter analysis is capable of articulating an overall theatrical code is indicated by studies already made in theater semiotics, specifically, in the recognition that there is an economy of theatrical signification, and a unique "transformability" in the formulation of theatrical signs.

A code can be more or less lucid, more or less immediately self-revelatory. Since the theatrical code is so heterogeneously constituted, furnished by both individual and social experience, by literary and artistic tradition, some of its messages display a high degree of variance between their points of emission and their points of reception. In every play, the ratio of signs perceived to signs emitted is established according to a host of variable factors: the spectator's general culture, his state of mind, his mental capacities, his physical condition, his physical position in the auditorium:[28] these, along with his degree of familiarity with the conventions being employed (his theatrical competence), render the operations of the theatrical code extremely problematic and aleatory. But the code recognizes this aspect of itself, and allows great flexibility in the coding operations. Thus all plays take a position somewhere between the two extremes of semiotic waste and semiotic parsimony, a choice made possible by the characteristic density and plurality of theatrical signification.

Semiotic waste takes many forms: by multiplying uses of the same sign, a message can use repetition and even redundancy to clarify itself. Often several signifiers can be associated with a single signified, as in Hamlet's famous antisemiotic statement:

> 'Tis not alone my inky cloak, good mother,
> Nor customary suits of solemn black,
> Nor windy suspiration of forced breath,
> No, nor the fruitful river in the eye,
> Nor the dejected havior of the visage,
> Together with all forms, moods, shapes
>   of grief
> That can denote me truly.

(act 1, sc. 2, lines 76–83)

Hamlet's melancholy is signified by a variety of signifiers from various subsystems: by costume, sound, expression, and by speech, the latter cleverly combining its usual informative and referential function with a semiotic one, underlining the nonverbal signs while claiming to outstrip them:

> But I have that within that passeth show
> These but the trappings and the suits of woe.

(lines 85–86)

At the other extreme, semiotic economy can reduce simultaneity, presenting signs one at a time, throwing each into stark relief to achieve its full significative potential without any disturbance. The extreme case of semiotic parsimony is perhaps the use of the so-called "zero sign," the pointed absence of a sign belonging to one of the subsystems. Thus silence is a zero sign of the speech system, capable, as Pinter has shown, of articulation into a sophisticated rhetoric of signification. Similarly, darkness is a zero sign of the lighting system, and can have both semantic (//blindness//, //despair//)[29] and syntactic (//end of a scene//) significance.

The theatrical code operates within these two extremes. For every signified in the message, it is capable of emitting signifiers from all its subsystems of signification, but it restricts this potentially total plurality in order to balance emission and perception, and to highlight the most productive signs. (For instance, all speech could be accompanied by the full repertoire of pantomimic gestures, but usually only certain ones are employed.)

The second characteristic feature of the theatrical code is the transformability of its signs. Curiously enough, the theater, a highly mimetic art and one consequently capable of great iconic signification, employs a large number of cross-mediational signs, signs of which the signifier and the signified belong to altogether different existential realms. For example, a great number of *object*-signifieds can be signified not just by object-signifiers (e.g., a real chair signifies //chair//) but by acoustic ones: //rain// can be signified by /the sound of water splashing/, a //car arriving// by /the sound of tires screeching/, a //war// by /the sound of machine guns firing/. Thus the stage is denoted not just spatially—the actual set we see—but also acoustically—the sounds we hear.[30]

The acoustic sign provides only one instance among many of this transformability. Spatial elements can also be signified by light (as when spotlights go on and off different groups on stage to indicate simultaneous action in different locales: a semiotic trait exploited thematically in Beckett's *Play*), by movement and gesture (the classic mimed door), by props (two pillars metonymically signify a palace, a throne signifies a royal court), by writing (Brecht's posters), and by speech ("This is the forest of Arden"; Shakespeare's plays abound with such space-speech transformations, and his Edgar's description of the Cliffs of Dover to blind Gloucester is the finest metasemiotic use of the phenomenon). The actor is a particularly flexible signifier, and can perform a variety of stage functions (as distinct from acting functions). He can be a place (the human trees of the wood in Dürrenmatt's *The Visit*), a prop,[31] a piece of furniture,[32] an atmospheric phenomenon,[33] a geographical entity,[34] a nonentity.[35] Conversely, scenic elements can perform human or actor functions, as in the case of a mirror reflection (Laudisi's famous dialogue with his reflection in Pirandello's *It Is So (If You Think So)*), and of film projection showing a person or a group of people.[36]

Recognition of the transformability of the theatrical sign has frequently led to the illogical conclusion that a signified can be attached to a variety of signifiers without producing a concomitant transformation in the sign being constituted. This error represents a forgetting of the central axiom of semiotics: that a sign is the *combination* of a signifier and a signified, and cannot be identified solely with the one or the other. Thus when the signified //rain// is conveyed through the signifier /sound of water falling/ this constitutes a *different sign* from that achieved when the signifier employed is /actor entering in wet clothes/. To regard both these cases as the same *sign* is to confuse sign with signified. In fact, the choice of signifier is of paramount significance in the description of the theatrical message: to ignore it is to slip back into the nostalgia for uncoded meaning.

The transformability of the theatrical sign (Jindrich Honzl calls it "dynamics"; other writers have termed the phenomenon "mobility" and "transcodability")[37] is not merely a characteristic of the theatrical sign but a *rule* of the theatrical *code*. Many kinds of signs—including linguistic ones—are heteromaterial[38] (i.e., the "stuff" or "continuum" from which the signifier is fashioned is different from the stuff or continuum of its possible referent). Thus the verbal signifier /tree/ is made of ink marks, not of bark, leaves, etc., as is its referent «tree». Of course, not all signs are heteromaterial. There are homomaterial signs in which both the signifier and the possible referent are made of the same material. All ostensive signs, samples, and examples are of this type, as, for instance, when a single pointed-at or picked-up /cup/ is a sign for the class of objects //cups//. The important point, however, is that the hetero- or homomaterial nature of a sign is not a matter of free choice, but is dictated by a convention contained in the code. Thus only a specially inscribed piece of *paper,* /a bank note/, will be a sign for a certain amount of *gold;* a specially articulated *sound,* a spoken word, will be a sign for a certain supposed *object.* The code governing money, or the code governing language, contains within it, as part of its set of constituent rules, a specification about the continuums it will correlate.

Now, this is not the case in the theatrical code, which is why transformability is an aspect not of the sign but of the code. The theatrical code contains a *rule* which allows for "free" material correlation: it does not require that its signs be homomaterial *or* heteromaterial, far less that the heteromateriality be of a certain specified sort. Thus a //tree// can be signified by: /painted image of a tree/, /an actor with limbs outstretched imitating a tree/, /a steel and wire construction that looks like a tree/, and so on. Moreover, as various theater semioticians have pointed out, transformability does not have to be restricted even within a given play.[39] A signifier can "float" from one signified to another even during a single performance: the /piece of wooden furniture/ that stood for //a park bench// in scene 1 can stand for //a bed// in scene 2. (Again, it is worth emphasizing that in all these cases we are dealing with different *signs,* not merely different *signifiers.*)

This feature of theatrical signs would seem to point to a *lack* of code altogether, an effect that is characteristic of all art: "It is indeed difficult to avoid the conclusion that a work of art *communicates too much* and therefore *does not communicate at all,* simply existing as a magic spell that is radically impermeable to all semiotic approach" (emphasis in original).[40] The characteristic density of aesthetic texts (actually a result of "overcoding" at both levels of signification)[41] has given rise to the belief that their interpretation is largely a matter of "intuition," not of systematic "decoding." This notion is probably nothing more than a shortcut response to the *complexity* of the codes operating in aesthetic texts, codes that we are still a long way from isolating and analyzing. As Eco says, however, "there is some degree of philosophical laziness in merely labelling as 'intuition' every experience that demands an excessively subtle analysis in order to be described."[42]

Scrutiny of the park bench/bed reveals that, far from being uncoded or undercoded, the theatrical sign is overcoded: its meaning derives from its position in a structure of signs, from a set of relations between it and other elements in the scene. The /piece of wooden furniture/ attains the signified //park bench// through *combination* with a number of other signs: speech signs (/"Let's sit down and rest here for a moment"/), costume signs (/outdoor garb/), and character signs (/policeman/, /pair of lovers/). When some or all these other signs are changed, the furniture sign sustains a parallel transformation: it comes to stand for //bed// when it is combined with new speech signs (/"Lie down and get some sleep now"/), costume signs (/nightgown/), scenic signs (/door/, /window/), décor signs (/lamp/, /dresser/), character signs (/maid/). In other words, a theatrical sign, like a word, acquires or conveys meaning through certain rules about its replacement capacity (paradigmatic identity) and its combinational capacity (syntagmatic identity). Thus when a scene shifts from "public" space to "private" space, some of its signifiers acquire new signifieds and lose old ones: the "position" occupied by //a park bench// in the public space is filled by //a bed// in the private space, and this change is determined or governed by a set of rules for the constituting of such spaces (a code).

Thus the "freedom" or "magic spell" quality of aesthetic communication is an illusion: "This means that a work of art has the same structural characteristics as does a *langue*. So that it cannot be a mere 'presence'; there must be an underlying system of mutual correlations, and thus a semiotic design which cunningly gives the impression of non-semiosis."[43] Nevertheless, the "system" of a work of art *is* somewhat different from a linguistic system, and it is better to read Eco's analogy between the two as figurative rather than literal. The difference is that whereas *langue* is a collective and relatively stable system, the system underlying an artwork is largely an individualistic and constantly *emerging* or *dynamic* system. To deny the role of the individual author in forging this system is to risk reducing creative activity to a mechanical and deterministic "application" or "realization" of a preexisting system.

Theater, like all art, employs a code that is eternally making and remaking itself, and this is its semiotic uniqueness and character: "Through the close dialectical relationship maintained between message and code, the addressee becomes aware of new semiosic possibilities and is thereby compelled to rethink the entire language, the entire inheritance of what has been said, can be said, and could or should be said. By increasing one's knowledge of codes, the aesthetic message changes one's view of history and thereby *trains* semiosis" (emphasis in original).[44]

The transformability of the theatrical sign, which might also be termed the "unconstrained materiality condition" of the theatrical code, raises some other interesting questions. Of all communication systems, the theater would seem to be the one that could dispense altogether with heteromateriality in its signs. The heteromaterial theater sign seems to exist in an unnecessary or gratuitous opposition to a potentially perfect iconicity. Since very few things are, in principle, impossible to *duplicate* on stage, theatrical signification should, it would seem, be totally iconic. Indeed, "the theater is perhaps the only art form able to exploit what might be termed iconic *identity:* the sign-vehicle denoting a rich silk costume may well be a rich silk costume, rather than the illusion thereof created by pigment on canvas."[45] That is to say, the theater seems to have the capacity to employ signs of an even greater degree of iconicity than that found in those signs (painted images, icons) which have traditionally been considered the *most* iconic. This being the case, it would seem that iconic identity would be the *norm* in theatrical sign-production; instead, it is the exception. (If it were not so, audiences would not be as surprised and delighted as they are when a play incorporates a real dog, or includes the action of *really* frying an egg.) The expectation is that many elements *will* be artificially realized—so much so that a "natural" element is regarded as a violation of the code, and consequently "read" as such (thus being semiotized at another level).

The issue I have raised is part of one of the most debated and least understood areas of semiotics: the notion of iconicity. Iconicity is a veritable Pandora's box for semiotics, and has generated tremendous controversy ever since it was opened by C. S. Peirce, the founder of American semiotics.[46] Peirce, classifying signs according to a taxonomic principle of "modes of correlation," offered a tripartite typology of signs: the index (where signifier and signified are correlated by cause or contiguity), the icon (correlated by similitude), and the symbol or sign proper (correlated by convention). Of all these, the icon has proved most difficult and intractable, largely due to a lack of precision about what "similitude" means. Charles Morris paraphrased Peirce as follows: "a sign is iconic to the extent to which it itself *has the properties* of its denotata," later altering this to: "An iconic sign, it will be recalled, is any sign which is *similar in some respects* to what it denotes."[47] Even the modified definition, however, is extremely unsatisfactory; as Eco says: "if an iconic sign is similar to the thing denoted *in some respects,* then we arrive at a definition which satisfies common sense, but not semiotics."[48] The problem is that a close analysis of any sign that seems to resemble its supposed referent reveals the intermediary existence of some cultural *convention* defining the notion of "resemblance" or "similarity," thereby reducing the apparent iconicity of the sign to the status of an "illusion" of similarity, not "real" similarity. Eco proposes that the notion of iconicity be abandoned altogether, being a deceptive and inaccurate category that has functioned as a catchall for a variety of very different sign relations. (Peirce himself included, in the class of iconic signs, not just images, which are problematic enough, but also diagrams and *metaphors*! The latter inclusion is enough to show how useless the category is, for if metaphors are icons, then so also are words!)

What Elam is talking about in his "iconic identity" example of the rich silk costume may not be an icon at all, but a pseudoiconic phenomenon that Eco calls a "duplicative replica" or a "double."[49] The sense in which Eco uses the term "double" is radically different from its familiar literary sense ("doppelganger") which, in Eco's taxonomy, would not be a double but a partial replica. Eco's "double" is an object or sign that is produced in the exact same way (techniques, material, all specifications) and *for the same purpose* as another object. Thus a car that comes off the assembly line will be a "double" of the previous car on the line, but it will not be a *sign* for that other car. In fact, "doubles" are not signs of each other; the only case in which a double can function as a sign is when it is used as an ostensive sign, "picked up" to stand for all the members of its class[50] (actually, in such a case, it is no longer a double but an ostensive sign).

The /rich silk costume/ that stands for a //rich silk costume// would appear to be a double, in that it is produced in exactly the same way as a rich silk costume would be. However, Elam's terminology is inaccurate. The /rich silk costume/ does not stand for a "costume" (at least not in the theatrical sense) but for "clothes" (or "costume" in the social sense). Thus the two elements have different *purposes*; a real silk robe is worn by a real queen, while a silk costume is worn by an actress *in order to play the role* of a queen and signify this. This is why heteromateriality enters the theatrical realm: nothing on stage is there for the purpose it has in the (fictional) social realm of the play (the drama); rather it is there to *achieve* that fictional realm, its purpose is always *theatrical,* and it can (indeed it must) therefore go beyond mere duplication, which would frequently fail to fulfill that purpose. (A good example of this is the stage whisper, which would fail to signify "whispered information" if it were a real whisper—i.e., a double of social "whispers"—audible only to the character addressed.)

The heteromateriality of the theatrical sign is, therefore, not a "free" phenomenon, but rule-bound and coded, essential to the theatrical communication, and enforced by certain features of the theatrical system (such as distance between performers and spectators, spatial and temporal limitations, etc.). I will have more to say about theatrical "iconicity" later, as it is one of Genet's central concerns, and powerfully productive in his plays' semantic contents.

These features of theatrical activity: the combinative quality of theatrical signs, their economy, and their transformability, clearly indicate that the process of theatrical signification is not random or free, but systematic and rule-bound. They point to the existence of a theatrical *code,* amenable to analysis, like language, from the point of view of its articulation, syntax, and semantics. The analogy with language is also fruitful in confronting the final and most important question of a semiotics of the theater: the question of the nature and location of the semiotic unit, the object of semiotic analysis. Like linguistics, the semiotics of theater can constitute its subject on a tripartite model, using the linguistic concepts of *langage, langue,* and *parole.*[51]

Langage, or the linguistic faculty, resembles the idea of *theatricalness,* the essential and transcendent quality of theater which underlies all types of theatrical activity. This is the subject of much modern dramatic theory, and is typically researched in anthropological or psychological terms. In semiotic terms, it may correspond to some sort of "theatrical competence," but one even more basic and fundamental than the theatrical equivalent of linguistic competence, which involves familiarity with a *given* language (see *"langue"* below). The theatrical *langage* would be a kind of macrocode which constitutes theater *as such,* and sets the stage for the functioning of any given theatrical code or codes: "Performances can be properly understood only on the basis of a theatrical competence, more or less shared by performers and audiences, comprising familiarity with the kinds of codes and sub-codes we have been discussing. *But there is a more fundamental form of competence required before the spectator can begin to decode the text appropriately: the ability to recognize the performance as such"* (my emphasis).[52] The question "what is a play?" has traditionally received a historicist answer, in which drama is defined as an evolving form of originally religious activity: a secular ritual. A semiotic approach to the question must first restate it, as follows: "what is it that we recognize when we recognize a play as a play?" Posed in this way, the question takes its place in a larger inquiry, that of the conceptualization of social experience. It becomes part of the ubiquitous question that social scientists like Erving Goffman and Gregory Bateson have recognized as basic to all effective social behavior, the question "what is it that is going on here?" This question, as Goffman points out, is partly circular, for it suffers the vicissitudes of all inquiry that must be mediated by language. In this case, the terms "it," "going on," and "here" are already answered parts of the question being posed:

> To ask the question "what is *it* that's going on here?" biases matters in the direction of unitary exposition and simplicity....
> So, too, to speak of the "current" situation (just as to speak of something going on "here") is to allow reader and writer to continue along easily in their impression that they clearly know and agree on what they are thinking about. The amount of time covered by "current" (just as the amount of space covered by "here") obviously can vary greatly from one occasion to the next and from one participant to another.... [53]

The problematic of situation-definition is inherent in theater, where time, space, action, and person are all both real and unreal, actual and virtual.

How, then, do people answer the problematic question "what is it that is going on here?" According to Goffman, they do so by recourse to "frames," which are conceptual structures they impose on (or rather, "read into" *and* "out of") the flux of experience, and which comprise and contain the rules by which a portion of that flux (a "strip") becomes distinct, intelligible, and negotiable: "I assume that definitions of a situation are built up in accordance with *principles of organization which govern events*—at least social ones— and *our subjective involvement in them;* frame is the word I use to refer to such of these basic elements as I am able to identify. That is my definition of frame" (emphasis mine).[54]

Frames are social, not individual, constructs, and "frame analysis" is, consequently, a semiotics. Thus when Goffman analyzes the "theatrical frame," his discoveries closely resemble what theater semioticians have identified as the essential rules governing signification in the theater: the theatrical macrocode. These rules are, as it happens, one of the central themes or concerns of Genet's play *The Blacks,* so that I shall reserve my discussion of them until my chapter on that play.

Langue, or the language (such as English or French), would correspond to types of theater (e.g., Occidental, Oriental), as well as to smaller subdivisions of these by genre (tragedy, comedy, farce, etc.) and period (Greek tragedy, Elizabethan tragedy, modern tragedy, etc.). Each of these groups could provisionally be regarded as an institution, a set of interpersonal rules and norms, and seen to be capable of description in semiotic terms. I say "provisionally," because there is no guarantee that the types of theater identified by semiotic analysis will coincide with the types identified by literary tradition. It is entirely possible, even probable, that one of the effects of a semiotic approach to theater will be to dissolve previous classifications (e.g., by genre, by period, by place) and construct new ones (by, for instance, predominance of certain kinds of signs).

Moreover, recalling my discussion of the dynamic (code-making) nature of aesthetic texts, it will be clear that the various types of theater ("genres," "movements," etc.) are neither fixed nor complete. It is characteristic of theatrical movements or types that they are often temporary categories, that they are in flux, and that they are never discrete, mutually exclusive entities. Also, they often *seem* to be constituted after the fact, products of critical rather than creative activity; but the lag between their use and our recognition and description of them need not disqualify them from the class of signifying systems.

Parole (or the actual manifestations of the language by individuals who have mastered it) would correspond to the actual dramatic works, by individual authors, which constitute the (open) set of any one type. Semiotic theory would occupy itself with these individual manifestations and (or in terms of) their relationship to the group to which they seem to belong. Thus a play like *The Balcony,* and perhaps all the other dramatic works by the same playwright, would be decoded in terms of the institution "modern drama" or "avant-garde drama," a process which could change and would certainly narrow down this initial classification, at the same time as it would contribute to the articulation of a general code used by the institution in question.

Unfortunately, several problems accompany this application of the linguistic model to theater, all contingent on the peculiar nature of the institution. The first problem arises out of the fact that drama, intended for performance, can be said to *manifest* itself not as a fixed text but as a repeatable and variable process. It is wrong, many modern scholars would argue, to think that the *parole* of drama is the playscript—rather, one might designate this as the *langue* of which the various productions are the *paroles*. (Why stop here? One might regard a production as the *langue*, and the different performances, night after night, as *paroles*.) What is at stake here is the very *object* of theater semiotics; without consensus on what will be, and can be, studied in this way, research is either paralyzed or succumbs to ruminations on "the essence of theater" (and that way, if not madness, certainly impasse lies). In such a case, it becomes necessary to overcome our timorousness and arrogate to ourselves the responsibilities of a theoretical choice.[55]

If it is to be a theory that avoids the pitfalls of traditional "literary" dramatic theory, semiotics must certainly not restrict itself to a study of dramatic texts, or rather of the linguistic component (the dialogue) of these texts. On the other hand, any attempt to situate analysis at the opposite extreme—that of actual, individual performance—is to incur all the liabilities of its inherently evanescent and largely aleatory nature. The analogy with film is instructive in this respect: although film is, like theater, a heterogeneous system whose various sign systems are deployed both temporally and spatially, a film is a fixed product: its various "viewings" can no more qualify it as a process than the various readings of a novel can deny its "product" nature. A film is like a book: it has a physical existence, it is capable of division into discrete segments for the purpose of prolonged scrutiny. The performance of a play is a process, and its unfolding in time is a primary, not secondary condition of its existence. To arrest this temporal flow is to deprive a play of its existence; "frame" analysis of the kind performed by film semiotics is unavailable in the theatrical medium, although it is approximated in analyses of the photographic records of a production. Such analyses necessarily exclude not only consideration of, but also response to, such important simultaneous signs as sound, movement, and speech. They employ a focus, duplicated also by the camera angle and distance of each shot, which distorts the object of study.

To solve this problem, it is necessary to mediate between the extremes of literary and performance analysis. We may do this by positing the stable existence of a text that, while it is *recorded* in the playscript, consists of information relating not only to verbal signs but also to nonverbal ones. This text might simply be called "the text," were it not for the traditional connotative restrictions of that word to mean "the words" or "the book" of the play. An alternative term, "Performance-Text," encounters other problems: the term has sometimes been used to mean "performance being studied." Since what I have in mind is neither just the script nor an actual performance but rather a *virtual* entity, constructed or posited for the purpose of semiotic analysis, which includes both verbal as well as nonverbal elements of a play, I will coin a term to refer to it: the T-Text (or "Total Text"). The T-Text may be defined as the set of *all* signs, from both verbal and nonverbal systems of signification, which the author includes directly or referentially in his script, and which he intends its production to employ. It is all the information provided by the playwright, through stage directions, in the dialogue, as well as by other means (prefaces, prologues, letters, typographical conventions, manuscript form, etc.). It therefore includes his indications about performative elements such as stage design, décor, costume, movement, gesture, light, and sound.

The concept of a T-Text has the virture of defining and delimiting the object of study, but it is bound to be rejected by many theater practitioners, especially by directors, whose creativity it might appear to restrict or even deny. But this is not the case: to attribute more than pure literary activity to playwrights is not just fair and reasonable, but also necessary to any real description of their special practice; at the same time, it is by no means to assert that the performance is *totally* controlled by the playwright, for the signs he requires will always be differently realized by various productions. Thus, the T-Text of *Waiting for Godot* calls for a bare tree, but leaves the stage designer of any given production to decide whether this tree will be realistic or stylized, made of wood or cardboard, colored brown or pink. The aesthetic quality of a production will derive from the coherence of various choices made in realizing the required signs, but the dramatic significance of the play will be based on the proper inclusion of all the signs indicated by the T-Text. (Didi and Gogo under a red fiberglass tree is permitted by the T-Text; Didi and Gogo under a lamppost is not.)

At this point it might be objected that the author's text is far from sacred. Indeed, since Artaud's "No More Masterpieces,"[56] the directorial "interpretation" of plays, which might include editing, restructuring, and even changing central signs (the ghost of Hamlet's father replaced by a willful radio!), has become a cherished value in our theaters. The notion of a T-Text might, in fact, function as a kind of theoretical norm against which these interpretations could be measured and assessed—perhaps opening up a subfield of theater semiotics, a semiotics of the performance options of individual texts. But a more important function such a notion would perform is to distinguish between performances of a play and adaptations of it. Once a production engages in wholesale renovation of the signs contained in a play, it moves out of the first category and into the second, and creates a new T-Text (thus Charles Marowitz's Macbeth is not Shakespeare's play, and is properly entitled *The Marowitz Macbeth;* the same is true of Grotowski's *The Constant Prince,* and many others). The distinction is important. A production can be true to the text or an eccentric distortion of it; the latter may have a value of its own, but this foreign value ought not to be attributed to the original, nor added to its signification. If a director chooses to have Genet's Blacks wear white makeup instead of the white masks Genet explicitly calls for, he is diverging from a signification obviously important to the author. Of course, he is free to do so, but his practice should not be regarded (except, perhaps, negatively) as part of the signification of Genet's text. Interestingly enough, one of the most vocal advocates of the sanctity of a dramatist's text is Genet himself. His notorious reaction to the London production of *The Balcony,* by Peter Zadek, was not restricted to words. He actually stormed onto the stage and tried to have the performance stopped.[57] He later justified this extreme behavior in an interview: "Imagine that my stage directions require a dumb show in front of the Arc de Triomphe . . . does the producer have the right to bring on a full chorus from the Paris Opéra? The dramatist has a duty to see that his play is treated with proper respect. This is not a question of divergences in interpretation; it's downright attempted murder!"[58]

It will be remarked that some plays furnish denser T-Texts than others. Thus, Shaw's plays seem to incorporate, through lengthy prefaces and stage directions, many more references to the non- and paraverbal signs to be used in their productions than do, say, Beckett's. The difference, however, is one of degree only, for a close analysis of the dialogue of sparsely annotated texts like Beckett's and Shakespeare's reveals a host of nonverbal signs, which could not be excluded in performance without seriously distorting the text's significance. Modern drama theorists have shown how this feature of dramatic texts, always tacitly known to directors and actors, can successfully be made to serve critical analysis and interpretation. Dramatic dialogue is not simply the carrier of thematic meaning but also the container of very specific theatrical signs. Besides being read to interpret a character's psychological and philosophical makeup, it can also be used to envision this character's physique (Cassius is lean), expression (and "hungry looking"), movement (Gogo limps), spatial context (Juliet's balcony), and so on.

T-Texts differ not only in density but also in their extension. While some restrict themselves to indicating stage signs only, others move beyond the stage to the physical structure and characteristics of the theater itself (Genet explicitly asks that *The Screens* be performed outdoors) and the audience

(*The Blacks* requires at least one white spectator, even if only in effigy). These cases illustrate the relationship of T-Text to performance: productions are often limited in a number of ways from following all the playwright's instructions (*The Screens* has usually been performed indoors, for lack of availability of an open amphitheater), and must improvise. These limitations should not affect dramatic analysis, however—the T-Text stands by itself, and has an internal coherence. Secondly, the extension of some T-Texts over others shows that areas controlled in one case may be "free" in others: most plays can be performed in a variety of different types of auditoriums (although the choice is normally restricted somewhat by other conventions of the piece: the episodic "tableau" form of "epic" theater militates against too "intimate" a staging and many realistic-psychological plays "get lost" in huge auditoriums). This simply means that performance texts are of different kinds, not that some accommodate semiotic analysis while others do not. Even textless or authorless plays like those performed by the Open Theater and the Living Theater have T-Texts, recorded in unorthodox ways.

The recognition of such an entity as the T-Text, or, if you will, the construction of such an object for the purposes of semiotic analysis, is a first step towards creating a theater semiotics comparable in theoretical scope and practical applicability to the advanced semiotics of literature and film. But the semiotics of theater may develop also along another line, one furnished by the specifically theatrical or reflexive mode of much avant-garde theater. While theater semiosis is clarified through close analysis of various T-Texts, several of these texts supplement this analysis by providing a semiotic analysis of their own. Indeed, insofar as modern drama is metatheatrical it is also semiotic; and insofar as he shares the semiotician's concern with signification the modern playwright is also a semiotician: his plays are, at one and the same time, messages in a theatrical code, and explorations of that code.

This double focus is clearest, perhaps, in the work of playwrights who are also theoreticians, playwrights like Bertolt Brecht, whose semiotic concerns not only structure his theory of performance but also constitute, according to Roland Barthes, the central theme of all his drama: "What Brechtian drama as a whole postulates is that today at least, drama has not to express the real so much as to signify it."[59] Brecht's plays, that is to say, are not merely semiotic objects (which all plays are) but also semiotic analyses, formulating, in the course of signification, the principles and conditions of a special kind of signification.

The same is true of Genet's drama; it, too, is both semiotic object and semiotic analysis, an artistic-theoretical structure which explores its own codes. The semiotician who confronts Genet finds, therefore, that the playwright frequently moves out of the frame of analysis and joins the analyst in decoding the theatrical message. As playwright, Genet employs a host of signs and functions; as semiotician, he theorizes about the theatrical process, explores its communicative possibilities, and specifies the nature of its signs. In this latter role he equals Brecht, although his semiotic concerns are manifested less formally, not in theoretical writings but in frequent and impassioned responses to productions, advice to directors,[60] and elaborate stage directions. These scattered but powerful statements of principle combine with his metatheatrical themes to create a nonsystematic semiotics of theater.

It is at these two levels that I propose to approach two of Genet's plays: to read them as inscriptions in a special code, utilizing the special signs of this code, and as analytic explorations of the principles of theatrical signification, inquiries into the social and psychological foundations of theatrical communication. My reasons for this dual focus are of primary importance: I hope to show that the plays' semiotic *"theme"* is a central element of their code, indeed, that semiotic analysis is the *mode* of avant-garde theater, not just one of its subsidiary concerns, that without it the avant-garde message could not be formulated. The semiotic theme is, in short, what makes it possible for the "impossible theater" to communicate itself without destroying itself.

3

The Balcony

Avant-Garde Drama and Deconstruction

What is the disturbing? Above all, that which does not declare itself as such.

Barthes, *Obliques*

The authenticity of a drama of denial depends upon its ability to uproot and destabilize—in theatrical terms—the preexisting conditions of dramatic signification. This uprooting must be performative, that is, it must *be*, not simply be discussed, referred to, or declared. The avant-garde drama of impossibility—which, as I will show, is really the drama of postmodern[1] perception and communication—must be coded in opposition to the familiar and accessible system established by preceding theatrical practice. A failure to realize the radical code in performance leads to the kind of neutralization of the theatrical message that Barthes laments in his review of Peter Brook's production of *The Balcony*: "Today Genet is suffering the fate of all avant-garde theater, which is irretrievably neutralized from the day it is acknowledged by the audience from whom it sought to break off... One can say that *The Balcony* is accomplishing an inflexible law: it was inevitable that Genet would one day be accepted: that day has come."[2] The law that Barthes speaks of, a kind of Marcusian law of one-dimensionality, which says that radicalism in art as in politics can be destroyed by being coopted by its intended targets, is perhaps not as inevitable as Barthes so fatalistically imagined. It appears to be so, especially in the theater, where the radical artist is bound by necessity to use the historically derived means of contact with the audience, for to break or ignore them would be to forfeit the possibility of communication altogether. Nor is the avant-garde playwright alone in this predicament: he shares it with all those artists, writers, philosophers—even anthropologists, political scientists and psychologists—who have become aware of the need for their discourse to take responsibility for itself.

Since Heidegger, philosophy, and along with it other disciplines, has become intensely self-conscious, recognizing the heavy charge of tacit, assumptive, precomprehended premises which underlie and shape its inquiry. The inescapable nature of these shaping biases appears strongly when it is realized that they permeate our language and are embedded in its very structure. The ideological structure of language converts this supposed *instrument* of knowledge into a *kind* of knowledge itself, a prison-house within which we are trapped instead of a tunnel of escape into objective reality. Thus the language we possess possesses us.

The recognition of this problem, however, can be a first step toward resolving it. Like all contradictions, this one lends itself to a dialectical development, an escape from the prison which is not at the same time a forgetting of it.

It is the spectacle of just such an escape, in fact, that Genet's drama confronts us with. His plays are the theatrical versions of a mode of discourse increasingly familiar in philosophical and critical writings: deconstruction. His theater has the same effect, or performs the same tasks that Jacques Derrida claims all discourse must perform in order to unfold the structures that imprison us.

Interestingly enough, one of the most dramatic—and sophisticated— examples of deconstructionist critical practice happens to be Derrida's work on assorted Genet texts, in his notorious book *Glas*.[3] The notoriety of *Glas* is a function not only of its content but also—and primarily—of its structure and presentation, which are, to say the least, unusual. The text of *Glas* consists of (at least) two parallel and interrelated discourses, printed side by side in different typeface: in the left-hand column, Derrida conducts an analysis of and commentary on Hegel, focusing largely on his concept of the family and paternal authority; in the right-hand column, a similar discourse is woven around fragments of Genet's writings. Thus Derrida explores—allusively, circuitously—the lines of force, inscribed in the very sounds and structures of words and phrases, that link and separate the philosopher of "Right" and the criminal artist. *Glas* makes use of Genet, as a writer but mainly as a phenomenon, in a philosophical-literary experiment; it is not a study of his work(s) or an analysis of his methods. Moreover, it explores Genet's use of language exclusively. For these reasons, it lies outside the critical problematic surrounding Genet's drama, which is my major concern.

The parallel I find between Genet's plays and deconstructionist discourse warrants a short discussion of the latter, but does not, I feel, require the adoption of a deconstructionist method like Derrida's for describing Genet's practice. The following brief comments on philosophical and literary deconstructionism are offered, then, simply by way of analogy, as a clarification not of my method, but of Genet's.

The philosopher's solution to the problem of language as both instrument and kind of knowledge has been to confront and integrate the contradiction into his discourse. The technique employed to achieve this, instituted by Heidegger and elaborated more recently by Jacques Derrida, is that of writing *"sous rature"* or "under erasure."[4] The technique involves writing a word, crossing it out, and then printing both word and deletion. Thus Heidegger, seeking to preserve in his discussion of Being the fact that this question was *always* and of itself *already* answered (for to attempt to *define* Being is to employ the structure of definition—"Being *is*"—and therefore entails a prior acceptance of Being ("is")), put the word /Being/ "under erasure": ~~Being~~. Heidegger preserves the old word, because to invent a new one here would be "to risk . . . forgetting the problem or believing it solved."[5] The word is both inadequate and necessary, a rather tortuous predicament captured by the typographical form "word + deletion." Writing under erasure is the method of postmodern philosophy, which must "deconstruct" an entire heritage but is bound to do so in terms borrowed from that heritage itself.

The method of avant-garde theater is performance under erasure. Only by finding a way to both use and deny the old "language" of theater can the avant-garde escape the "inflexible law" Barthes speaks of, the law of one-dimensionality. Not all modern playwrights succeed in putting performance under erasure. When they do succeed, as Genet does, the mark of their success is a radical, total disunity. This disunity is much more than the existence of partial or temporary contradictions or ambiguities "ultimately incorporated into the text's system of unified meaning."[6] It is a *pervasive* and flagrant disunity, at the levels of character (self, personhood), staging (space), plot development (time, causality), dialogue (language), and structure (beginning, ending, center). It is an experience of the mystery of experience, a communication about the inadequacy of communication. In semiotic terms (which I will explore and explain below) it is a fall into the abyss between signifier and signified.

Viewed historically, the avant-garde can be seen as a synthesis of past and future. It occupies a present in which the future folds back on the past, a place in between but also including both the re-presented pseudopresent of the mimetic tradition and the presented theatrical present of the postmodern ideal.

Viewed semiotically, it conveys messages inscribed through the intersection of two codes, the conventional and the radical, the old and the new, the familiar and the unfamiliar. The content of this structural relationship between old and new codes, i.e., the nature of this avant-garde code, is primarily semiosic. The avant-garde message foregrounds its code, heightening the function which corresponds to the metalingual in Jakobson's communication model of the speech event. The avant-garde theatrical event is one in which message, context, and code overlap, are the same.

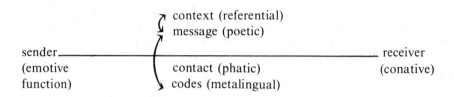

context (referential)
message (poetic)

sender—————————————————————— receiver
(emotive   contact (phatic)   (conative)
function)   codes (metalingual)

The avant-garde theater produces messages about (context) its own way of conveying messages (code). By constantly drawing attention to itself as theater, i.e., as a certain kind of system employing special types of codes, and by making a study of these codes one of its central messages, it creates itself *in terms of* traditional theater (which used some of the same codes) but also *in opposition to* traditional theater (in which those codes remained transparent, unacknowledged).

Thus, avant-garde theater both affirms and denies the traditional theater. In doing both, it duplicates the philosophical technique of writing "under erasure," presenting both the tradition and the rebellion, constructing a theatrical object which is "always already" deconstructed and which posits above all its lack of positive existence. To anticipate my discussion somewhat, I could say that the T-Text of *The Balcony* puts the stage itself under erasure, that what it creates, both experientially and theoretically, is the term/place: st̶a̶ge.

It may be well at this point to say a few words about the experience of erasure. The preceding discussion of the technique has the potential, by virtue of its abstraction, to signal a tortured, gloomy, and negative experience. As a critical tool, erasure threatens a reading of the plays which would reduce them to sterile intellectual investigations of a hopeless philosophical predicament. Indeed, there is no doubt that postmodernism frequently elicits a negative response by resolutely frustrating our desire for stable, positive, and final conclusions. Its systematic denial of univocality at all levels provokes a nostalgia for those old "truths" now revealed as fictions: the centered self, the objective world, the original word. But that this nostalgia is not the only possible response, indeed that it is the opposite of the appropriate one, has already been demonstrated by the postmodern rediscovery (and glorification) of Nietzsche,[7] the philosopher of "joyful unwisdom." Nietzsche's contribution to postmodern philosophy was the production of a new mode of philosophical discourse—the mode of "play," of constant risk, reversal, and subversion: "I do not know," wrote Nietzsche, "any other way of associating with great tasks than *play*."[8] Nietzsche's great contribution to philosophy is that of a mode, a method—his discourse proceeds deconstructively, subverting even itself at every successive stage. Derrida's translator speaks of Nietzsche's "pervasive strategy of intersubstituting opposites" in terms that will be particularly relevant to my discussion of Genet later: "If one is always bound by one's perspective, one can at least deliberately reverse perspectives as often as possible, in the process undoing opposed perspectives, showing that the two terms of an opposition are merely accomplices of each other."[9] The shifting of perspectives and the exposure of complicitous opposites is a hallmark of Genet's dramaturgy. Oppositions or shifts in perspective are, in fact, a characteristic of all drama, inscribed in the dramatic code in the form of its reliance on *dialogue*. Unlike the novel, the drama employs a discontinuous or pluralistic, instead of a continuous or singular, discourse, which makes it impossible for any one point of view to dominate and structure the whole. However, Genet's dramaturgy goes beyond this basic sort of perspectival shifting: in his works, it is not merely a matter of fluctuating between characters (and their world views) but of exposing the oppositional nature of *all* signs, concepts, and ideas. It is a matter of revealing the semiotically binary nature (signifier-signified) of all social and psychological experience. It is an insistence on the radical alterity at the heart of every entity.

Moreover—to return to my point about the experience of erasure—the theatrical (concrete) working out of this "compounding of opposites" is in Genet—as in Nietzsche—the opposite of gloomy or sterile. It is a dynamic and joyful process, where the intoxication of endless meaning-*production* far exceeds any disappointment we might feel at the lack of final meaning-*product*.

One last clarification before I go on to the text itself. The Nietzschean assault on binary opposition which I have just mentioned, and which characterizes post-Structuralist inquiries like Derrida's, may seem to be at odds with semiotics, the professed method of this inquiry, which has an opposition built into its core concept. The two parts of the sign—the signifier and the signified—are seen, in the original (Saussurian) formulation, to be inextricably linked, like the two sides of a sheet of paper. However, to Derrida, who is acutely aware of remnants of the positivist nostalgia for unity, for undivided *presence*, in modern thought, the Saussurian sign appears to harbor just such a nostalgia. His version of it, however, finds not a unity but a heterogeneity: "the other of the signified is never contemporary, is at best a subtly discrepant inverse or parallel... of the order of the signified."[10] What Derrida is alluding to here is the fact that the distance between word and thing (referent) is equally present between sound (or image)—the signifier—and concept—the signified. The sign does not bring forth "the presence of the signified... Word and thing or thought never in fact become one. We are reminded of, referred to, what the convention of words sets up as thing or thought, by a particular arrangement of words. The structure of reference works and can go on working not because of the identity between these two so-called component parts of the sign, but because of their relationship of difference. The sign marks a place of difference."[11] Difference, or *différance* (with an "a," Derrida's combinative neologism for the dual process of differentiation [difference] and deferment [postponement of meaning, from signifier to signifier])[12] is a significational phenomenon that Genet is familiar with; the semiosic theme of his plays repeatedly incorporates examples of it. Difference is, along with shifting perspective, confounded opposition, and deconstruction, the message as well as the method of *The Balcony*.

Deconstructing Theatrical Signs

Genet's Crucifix

A true postmodernist text, *The Balcony* is primarily engaged in semiotic exposure, change, and reversal. Its concern with theatrical semiosis is, moreover, performative, not merely philosophical, so that it makes its claim to genuine postmodernist communication through a process of *concrete, theatrical deconstruction*. It is an attack on theater and a satire of theatrical signifiers, a satire which eventually emerges as a full-fledged embodiment of postmodern thought and practice. A semiotic analysis of the play's performance-text reveals two main techniques that feed this process: one, a persistent semiotic theme, and two, a constant challenge to spatial stability.

The semiotic theme, which has broadly been called "metatheater," is in fact a systematic analysis of theatrical signs, an attempt to distinguish the specifically theatrical sign from other kinds (literary, social, etc.), and to define its nature. In this regard, perhaps the most telling of Genet's remarks on theater is one he made to Roger Blin at the time the latter was directing a production of Genet's last play, *The Screens*: "In the same way, don't let the Arab worker light a cigarette: the match flame not being able to be *imitated* on stage; a lighted match, in the audience or elsewhere, is the same as on stage. To be avoided."[13] Although Genet's emphasis on the word "imitated" may appear to signal a strong mimetic interest, the remainder of the remark should show that the very opposite is the case. Genet's insistence on including only the imitable in theater shows that he is concerned primarily with the *stage* object or sign, not its "real" counterpart. Whereas the mimetic theater strives to blur the distinction between the realms of theater and reality, Genet insists on maintaining—indeed, foregrounding—that distinction. He will admit only those signs which can be made to look *like signs*. Thus Genet declares war on iconicity. Where iconic signs enter,[14] their iconicity is quickly exposed: or rather, what is used in signification is the *gap* between their signifiers (form) and their signifieds (concept): in short, their difference.

The very first scene of *The Balcony* provides us with a vivid example of this characteristic concern and technique of Genet's. The sign in question is the "*huge Spanish crucifix, drawn in trompe l'oeil*"[15] on one of the three folding screens which make up the décor of scene 1. I will discuss the meaning of this sign in the logic of that scene's semiosic system later; for the moment I wish only to explore it as an emblem of Genet's postmodern interest in difference. The crucifix is, in the first stage of perception, a scenic sign with a religious connotation, helping to define the stage space before it as a sacristy.

However, there is something about this sign that deserves special attention and illustrates an important feature of aesthetic signs. It is this: the signifier or sign-vehicle of an aesthetic sign appears to be further segmented, divided into two parts, each of which is significant in its own right. Whereas many social signs signify their related concept regardless of the material form of their signifiers, the material form of the aesthetic signifier is in itself meaningful. "Using the everyday rules of a language I can utter a word in many ways, changing the pronunciation, stressing certain syllables differently, or altering intonation patterns; yet the word remains the same. But in aesthetic discourse every free variation introduced in 'uttering' the sign vehicle has a 'formal value.'"[16] (Which is to say, in fact, that such variation is not "free" but rule-bound, capable of being described in a more subtly segmented aesthetic code.) Eco provides another example, much closer now to the sign at hand—Genet's crucifix:

> A red flag on a highway or at a political meeting can be based on various differently manipulated matters in order to be grasped as an expression: but the quality of the cloth and the shade of red are in no way relevant. What is important is that the addressee detects /red flag/ . Yet a red flag inserted in a pictorial work of art depends, among other things, upon its chromatic quality, in order to be appreciated (and to convey its signification).[17]

Genet could easily have required the designer to use an actual crucifix; the fact that he specifically calls for a pictorially represented one shows that part of the meaning he wishes it to convey is that of //a representation// . The cross is thus a /sign/ of a //sign// . This is the second level of the sign's meaning, and the one in which it participates in the play's semiotic theme. At this level, it is a metasemiotic sign. Furthermore, although this meaning emerges at the second stage of perception, its importance is by no means secondary. It structures the space around the crucifix as an artificial (or constructed, represented) space, instead of a "real" one. What we see (or "read") here is //a facsimile of a sacristy// , not //a real sacristy// . The crucifix is only one of many examples of "metasemiotic" signs, but I chose it as an emblem of Genet's practice because of its special signifier—the trompe l'oeil technique, itself symbolic of a certain way of viewing and organizing the world.

Trompe l'oeil is the extreme of artistic "iconicity." Along with the other techniques of illusionism, of which it is the epitome, trompe l'oeil is to painting what realistic theater is to drama: the passionate pursuit of the impression of actuality. Like all illusionism, it is a virtuoso use of the pictorial techniques of *perspective* and *foreshortening,* and it is these, by implication, that Genet's crucifix undermines.

The *Penguin Dictionary of Art and Artists* defines perspective as "a quasi-mathematical system for the representation of three-dimensional objects in spatial recession on a two-dimensional surface, i.e., for the creation of an independent pictorial space as a microcosm of nature."[18] The perspectivist is, in a way, in the business of science fiction. His products are fictions of space supported by the science of geometry, or rather by a geometrical illusion or paradox, since perspective is based on the axiom that parallel lines never meet but always appear to do so. Its success depends upon another construction—that of a fixed, stable, and single point of view positioned outside the fictional space, commanding it. Psychologically speaking, perspective is an egocentric system, one which constitutes not one but two fictions in its every product: the onlooking subject, the perceived object.

The mathematical features of this system have had, since its discovery in the fifteenth century, far-reaching effects. According to one scholar, the development of perspective has transformed human perception and sense of space, promoting a "rationalization of sight."[19] William M. Ivins argues that perspective, leading to the foundation of modern geometry, which in turn provided the basis for modern engineering, was an important factor in the development of the modern world:

> ...the most marked characteristics of European pictorial representation since the fourteenth century have been on the one hand its steadily increasing naturalism and on the other its purely schematic and logical extensions. Both are due in largest part to the development and pervasion of methods which have provided symbols, repeatable in invariant form, for representation of visual awareness, and a grammar of perspective which made it possible to establish logical relations not only within the system of symbols but between that system and the forms and locations of the objects that it symbolizes.[20]

Basing his observations on Ivin's thesis, Richard Palmer argues that the spatialization of the world by the discovery of perspective, and its promulgation of the notion that everything in this world is measurable, reducible to logical relations, is the "genesis of modernity." Modernism, with its "man-centered view of life," is the outgrowth of the pictorial technique of creating microcosms of nature by positing a simple, static point of view outside that microcosm, looking at it: "Thus, the spatialization of vision has ramifications that extend beyond the world of art. It has metaphysical and epistemological implications. Modern man begins to dream of reducing everything to measurable terms, of making everything visualizable, i.e., spatial. And the mind, with its armory of mathematical symbols, better and more reliable than any ordinary language, nominates man as the absolute monarch of all things."[21]

Genet's crucifix in trompe l'oeil is, by virtue of its theatrical context, an attack on this illusionist modernism: for in the theater, a medium affording multiple points of view, the trompe l'oeil technique is powerless, its trickery too immediately apparent. (I say "too immediately" because the trompe l'oeil technique fulfills itself *at the moment it is recognized as trickery,* not during the process of its *illusionist success.* Though paradoxical, this is nevertheless true. The sign "coded" in trompe l'oeil is massively subversive, even self-subversive: it entails drawing its interpreter into a fiction and then exploding the fiction: the interpreter's pleasure lies not in being fooled but in finding out that he has been fooled.)

Genet's antimodernism, we will see later, extends into the metaphysical and epistemological realms Palmer mentions, as it does into the psychological realm of perspectival influence: "The overemphasis on space and extension tends to divide the world into observing subject and alien, material objects.... The line of development is direct between it and ego-psychology."[22] The world of perspectivism, the "modern world," is a world of binary oppositions: subject and object, self and other, mind and matter. It is a world where the self is the constituted subject, the ego, whole and complete and distinct from all around it. Genet's world, on the other hand, is one of extremely fluid, unstable identity. It is a world where identity is defined *in terms of,* rather than *in opposition to,* the material world. However, a full-scale description of Genet's philosophical and psychological postmodernism must wait, for my purpose here is to show how this postmodernism of his is realized in concrete, performative terms. It is to Genet's stage, therefore, that I must now turn.

In the light of what has just been said about the link between modernism and spatialization, the following discussion of the spatial semiotics of *The Balcony* may appear contradictory. Indeed, of all modern playwrights, Genet seems to put most emphasis on the visual aspects of theater—of which spatial organization is certainly one. However, his famous dictum that "In the world of the theatre, everything takes place in the visible world and nowhere else,"[23] does not implicate him in a modernist perspective. The visible world of Genet's theater is aggressively theatrical, pointedly antirealistic. His war on iconicity institutes a rupture between the stage and reality; never does it allow for the kind of reduced assimilation of the latter into the art that illusionism thrives on. The visual in Genet's theater is quite different from, sometimes even the opposite of, the "visualizable."

Genet's Balcony

The Balcony, writes Genet, is "a celebration of the Image and of the Reflection."[24] As a clue to the method and meaning of the play, this statement seems fairly vague and abstract—a mirror, in fact, in which various criticisms and ideologies have readily discerned their own reflections. A closer look at the statement reveals, however, that its tendency is towards the very opposite of abstraction: its two main terms—image and reflection—when apprehended not as a duality but as a progressive focusing on a single idea carry the utterance away from the ambiguity of the initial "image" towards a fairly specific reading of it. An image can be pictorial, rhetorical, poetic, imaginative, mental, oneiric, psychological, political, etc. A reflection, however, is a special sort of image, distinguished by a unique use of space. It is the *projection* of a thing onto a *reproductive surface,* such as a mirror. A reflected image requires the preexistence of a reflectable entity, not necessarily in time but in the process of its formulation. It is a cross-spatial entity, a thing that actually occupies two spaces at the same time, and would cease to exist if this spatial duality were ruptured. If it is a sign, it is one where signified and signifier face each other across empty space, an alteration of the usual contiguous and layered relationship of these two parts of a sign. But the specular reflection "does not stand *for* something else; on the contrary it stands *in front* of something else, it exists not instead of but because of the presence of that something" (emphasis in original).[25] Given the fact that a sign is defined as something that *stands for something else to somebody,* can we say that the specular reflection, which stands *because of* something else, is not a sign at all? It would seem that the only kind of specular reflection that is a sign is one in which I see *someone else* whom I cannot see directly but whose presence I can surmise from his reflection in the mirror. This reflection would then be an indexical sign, standing (*to me*) *for* the other person.

   The Balcony plays on precisely this significational ambiguity of specular reflections. On stage a mirror image is an indexical sign, but one which "stands for" a nonsemiotic experience *at the dramatic level* (i.e., the reflection of the character is not, *to him,* a sign of himself; it is only so to the onlookers—both actors and spectators). This feeds into the dramatic-theatrical opposition that structures *The Balcony,* and is a central symbol in the play's theme of postmodernist identity. The spatial and semiotic uniqueness of the mirror sign makes it a perfect symbol, as we shall see, for the spatial, semiotic, and philosophical themes of *The Balcony.*

   Where does *The Balcony* take place? What is the theatrical and ontological status of the places and spaces which not only make possible this "celebration of the Image" but also define its nature and delimit the area of its celebration? We could say, simply, that it takes place nowhere, or, to use Julia

Kristeva's phrase, that it "does not take (a) place,"[26] for this is, in fact, the case. However, this fact, which is the fundamental source of the play's meaning, is a theatrical fact, concretely realized. It is in its rigorous progression towards actual spatial nonexistence that the play communicates. A semiotic reading of the play must trace, therefore, the process of its treatment of space (as a semiotic system) and expose the means whereby the stage is erased, leaving behind only its image.

The movement is both diachronic (removing layers of spatial certainty scene by scene) and synchronic (reiterating at every moment the inherently conventional, unnatural aspect of the stage as a place). Thus the play provides both a syntagmatic (horizontal, linear, temporal, and causal) as well as a paradigmatic (vertical, simultaneous) message of illocality.

The balcony, a balcony, is Genet's paradigm of spatial ambiguity of all sorts. /The Balcony/ is not only the name of a *play*, but also of a *building*, which houses a *brothel*: a signifier with three signifieds. As the name for a building it appears fleetingly to be a rational sign, for the facade of Mme Irma's establishment is adorned by an actual balcony, one experienced at various theatrical levels in the course of the play: as *dramatic context*, as *scenery* (scene 6: "In the background, at some distance we perceive the facade of the Grand Balcony" (p. 55)), and as *stage space* (scene 8: "The scene is the balcony itself, which projects beyond the facade of the brothel" (p. 70)). However, this apparent rationality is limited to the dubious realm of synecdoche, rendered even more dubious—indeed, tending towards euphemism—since the "whole" in question is a brothel, a secret, private space in every way opposed to the open, public nature of a balcony.

The treachery of signifiers is further exemplified in Mme Irma's term for her brothel: she likes to call it a "house of illusions" (p. 34). As a name for a brothel, /the Balcony/ is unsuitable, but, as a name for a space of illusion it is entirely appropriate. A balcony is a liminal space par excellence, duplicating at the physical level the "in-between-ness" that an image or illusion has at the metaphysical level. Just as an illusion is not a thing yet not nothing either, so a balcony is not an enclosed space, nor yet an open one. It exists at the intersection of inside and outside, open and closed, above and below. It is, in structural terms, an excrescence of structure into nonstructure, in physical terms, of locality into the void, in metaphysical terms, of being into nothingness. Its structural and physical status as paraspace makes it the perfect (and perfectly ambiguous) example of "being-there" (*être-là*), wherein being is both a function and condition of spatial location, but is being *there*, not *here*—that is, being as a reflection thrown outside, a projection.

The functional potentiality of a balcony further extends its ambiguity: it can be a prison, though open, an escape route, though closed, a vantage point, a lookout, a showplace. As a psychological space, it can be the locus of vertiginous despair and suicide, of desire and admiration and display, of power and authority, even, as in Genet's play, of symbolic murder. Its performative versatility flows from its curious combination of structural openness (vulnerability) and closeness (protection, security), and from its location at the intersection of the axes of height and width. Precariously occupying the point where the horizontal meets the vertical, combining in itself the connective powers of corridor (horizontal) and stairway (vertical), it is a space that marks spatial *relationships*, a place of difference.

The structural relativity and functional plurality of the balcony make it the perfect setting for a drama of negation (erasure). Although its instability is revealed only gradually, the revelation depends upon preexisting, pretheatrical significance which can later be made to bolster a more specifically theatrical spatial semiotics. For the moment, it is sufficient to say that Genet sets the stage for his attack on realistic, representational theater by equating his dramatic space with an unstable architectural space—a balcony. It is a reflection of this no-man's-space that he will (de)construct his no-man's-stage.

Space and Costume

The illocality of *The Balcony*, already foreshadowed by the instability of that name as sign and that place as space, begins to be rendered in theatrical terms as soon as the play begins. The stage space of scene 1 is pointedly *the same and different* from that of the following four scenes. By manipulating various signs, intensifying some while weakening others, retaining some intact while changing others, Genet calls into question not only the theatrical location but also the dramatic status of the activities that take place before us.

He takes his first step in this direction by exposing the perennial contradiction, or difference, between stage space and dramatic place, i.e., between the actual stage area we see and the fictional, illusory, or "virtual" place it is supposed to be. This contradiction, which the mimetic theater has always combatted by recourse to a detailed disguise of the former to look like the latter (i.e., by realistic staging, which uses a whole panoply of "iconic signs" to force the stage to resemble real life), is, in *The Balcony*, rapidly foregrounded.

Rapidly, but not immediately. For it is not until scene 1 changes to scene 2—a scene-change effected in full view, acknowledging itself as a *scene-* (i.e., not a *place-*) change—that a duality between two kinds of signs—dramatic signs and theatrical signs—appears. As the décor of scene 1 begins to move "from left to right, as if it were plunging into the wings," and as "the following set then appears" (p. 13), it becomes apparent that only part of the décor—the part that moves out—was specific to scene 1. Another part, consisting of two signs, remains in place, thus detaching itself from the décor of scene 1. Thus what was originally seen as a coherent, unified whole appears now to be two unequal parts, belonging to two different systems. The décor of scene 1—made up of red screens and containing certain costumes, actors, and actions—appears now in opposition to the two signs which do not change. These are the chandelier (always referred to in the stage directions as "the same chandelier") and the mirror (also "the same").

The system to which these two signs belong is the *dramatic or fictional system*: i.e., they define the fictional *place* (the brothel) within which the *spaces* of illusion, the studios, form a *theatrical system*. The dramatic signs accrue, by virtue of their permanence and persistence, a greater degree of solidity and reality than the theatrical signs, which, in contrast, appear all the more artificial, temporary, and fragile. Thus, at the very first scene change, Genet establishes one of the premises of his play, out of which his semiotic and spatial themes will be developed. This premise states that the theatrical realm (here signified by the moveable décor of scene 1) *is contained within* a dramatic realm (here signified by the chandelier and the mirror). Since this premise will have to be referred to several times during the ensuing analysis, and will be expanded, it is worth giving it a shorthand formulation, as follows: T ⊂ D (where T = theatrical; D = dramatic; ⊂ = "is contained within"). I shall return to this momentarily.

The persistence of the chandelier provides an occasion to introduce and perhaps offer a solution to one of the knottiest problems of theater semiotics: the problem of a sign's duration. Since the theater is a multilayered system of signification, one of the few artistic systems that unroll in *both* space and time, its signs appear to lack the kind of clarity and force that belong to signs of systems using only *one* organization, spatial or temporal. In music, notes are struck one after another; in painting, forms are deployed one beside the other; even in film, frames are seen one after another, each complete in itself. In the theater, however, signs exist in both space (set, costume, light) and time (speech, acting, etc.), simultaneously. The question therefore arises as to what makes a theatrical sign signify, and when.

Genet's chandelier provides a sort of answer: it shows that theatrical signs have a certain capacity for variable signification; they can be weakened or intensified at different moments without thereby being changed. Since most scenes put most of their signs on view from the outset, they are obliged at certain times to reactivate, or intensify, the signifying activity of one of these already present signs. A scenic sign like the chandelier, or the crucifix in scene 1, while forming part of the message from the start, may not be called upon to make its particular signifying contribution until well into the scene. Achieving the intensification itself is no problem—in the multicodal system of theater, it is a matter of shifting the signifier of a sign belonging to some other system (speech, gesture, light) to correlate with the signifier of the sign to be intensified. Nor does the newly intensified sign constitute a new sign: it is the sign it was from its earliest appearance, only its role in the message has been strengthened for the moment.

Thus the /chandelier/, while (weakly) signifying //opulence//, //formality//, //beauty//, etc., from the outset, gains a special *structural* or *spatial* signified—opposing its own permanence to the transient, temporary quality of the "sacristy"—when the scene changes. Its intensity of significance rises sharply at this point, and it gains a signified belonging to a different plane (the theatrical) from its original one (the social). Now the chandelier ceases to be mere décor, and becomes a place marker, a sign that allows Genet to distinguish between the (permanent) dramatic place—the brothel—and the (temporary) theatrical space—a studio or stage within the brothel.

At the moment of its intensification, the chandelier sign also participates in the all-important semiotic theme of the play. By temporarily assuming, as I have shown, a higher degree of permanence and "reality" than the rest of the décor, it soon makes a paradoxical point: it shows us that in the theater no scenic element is "mere" décor—it is always a sign—and, at the same time, it declares the opposite: all objects, even the most apparently real, are *signs* of some theatrical system. The chandelier, no matter how "real" it may seem (in contrast to the flimsy, moveable screens), is a sign of the décor system; it is, all appearances to the contrary, "mere" décor!

Thus the chandelier participates in Genet's semiotic theme, other examples of which fill the play. In scene 1, for instance, the stage direction calls for a chair, on which are draped "a pair of black trousers, a shirt, and a jacket." These garments exist in opposition to the costume already on the "Bishop," just as the permanent chandelier exists in opposition to the moveable screens. The /everyday clothes/ function as deceptively "natural" or "real" elements, and are used to intensify the semiotic (//costume//) nature of the Bishop's /costume/. The intensification is strongest in scene 3, where verbal and gestural signifiers are used to "detach" the /real clothes/ sign and reactivate its significance:

> THE GENERAL (*He points to the hat, jacket, and gloves*): Have that cleared out.
> IRMA: It'll be folded and wrapped.
> THE GENERAL: Have it removed from my sight.
> IRMA: It'll be put away, even burned.
>
> (p. 21)

At this point, again paradoxically, the client's clothes appear to be both "real" (as opposed to his costume) *and false,* since they are seen to be functioning as (iconic) signs of the costume system. On stage, all garments are costumes, no matter how closely they resemble real clothes.

The Balcony provides a number of such wrenchings of signs (signs belonging to a variety of subsystems) out of the dramatic and into the theatrical realm. The most interesting of these are perhaps the actors themselves, who all play two parts: the part of a dramatic character and then of that character playing a role. Thus the Balcony's clients are played by actors who play characters playing the roles of Bishop, Judge, and General. The most pointed example of an actor revealing himself—through an intermediary pretense of "real" (dramatic) existence—as being an actor, a sign, is Arthur, the pimp who first "plays" an executioner and then is killed, transformed into "a corpse," "lying on a kind of fake tomb of fake black marble" (p. 60). This dramatic death is intensified in discussion, only to reveal, paradoxically, its essentially fake, theatrical nature:

> IRMA: It's make-believe these gentlemen want. The minister desired a fake corpse. But this one is real—look at it: it's truer than life.
>
> (p. 61)

The corpse is "truer than life" in the sense usually associated with mimetic theater, which seeks to present not an alternative to life but a clearer, sharper image of it than is normally seen by us as we live it. The force of that clear image depends, however, on a supporting framework of fictional conventions, conventions that must be, and must remain, transparent and tacit. Genet's punning insistence on the lifelikeness of Arthur's death, however, attacks those conventions and pushes the audience to drop its willing suspension of disbelief. The pun, along with other blatantly theatrical signifiers (the fake tomb, the actor's immobility), converts this /death/ into a theatrical sign, signifying not //death// but //pretense// , and thereby disrupting and negating the dramatic message of which it was a part (the fictional Arthur's fictional death).

The Balcony is filled with such examples of semiotic exposure, most of which have been pointed out by critics from the "metatheatrical" school. I will not, therefore, dwell on them. Their importance to my argument lies in their role in the dialectic of dramatic and theatrical signs that I have been discussing. I have shown how Genet begins by establishing, early in the play, the premise $T \subset D$. The semiotic theme takes this premise a step further, making it $T^1 \subset D \subset T^2$. The obvious circularity of this model is entirely intentional, for although a distinction can be made between T^1 (the theatricality, of Mme Irma's studios) and T^2 (the theatricality of theater per se), the two are increasingly identified, expanding towards each other till they overflow into and flood the middle term—dramatic. To put it another way, *The Balcony* develops as a double-barreled attack on or invasion of the fictional/dramatic/"real"/illusionist content by the actual/theatrical/"fake" form, an attack so thoroughly successful that, as we shall see, it completely destroys the former and establishes the latter in its place.

The semiotic theme of *The Balcony* is the means whereby Genet escapes the paradox of negative affirmation, finding in this theme a way to affirm the theatrical by denying the dramatic. By endlessly refusing to grant theatrical preeminence to the fictional level of his play, by repeatedly rendering it as unstable and artificial at the theatrical level, he combats the idea of a play as a re-presentation, an afterimage reflecting some prior meaning emanating from some absent creative consciousness. In so doing he creates a theater of presence, in the present, a theatrical message in a theatrical code instead of a literary message translated into theater.

The Spatial Semiotics of *The Balcony*

The chandelier in the play's early scene is, then, a sign with at least two (levels of) signifieds: it signifies spatial constancy, and by a development of this signification, it also signifies its own semiosic nature (i.e., that it is a décor *sign,* not a "real" chandelier). It is to the first level of signification, the spatial level, that I wish now to return.

The chandelier (and the mirror) remains "the same" in the first three studio scenes and then in the scene in Mme Irma's chamber. They function, then, as fixed elements of a spatial structure which seems to change, to revolve, to be a succession of places, but is, because of them, not a spatial syntagm but a paradigm. Their continued presence transforms the appearance of difference to a statement of sameness. This sameness is a sameness of identity, not merely of resemblance, at least not in the first three scenes, where we see quite plainly that this is the *same* chandelier, not just another one exactly like it (this is not necessarily true of the mirror).

Does this same chandelier make studios one, two, and three aspects of the same space, a single room redecorated in three different ways? Certainly this seems to be implied in the Bishop's remark:

> THE BISHOP: What you mean is that you need the room for someone else and you've got to arrange the mirrors and jugs.
>
> (p. 12)

Irma does not confirm this, and neither does Genet. The method of scene change he requires contradicts this possibility. A more conventional scene change, in darkness, could easily convey the kind of spatial identity the Bishop suggests. Instead, Genet insists that scenes 1 and 2 occupy different theatrical spaces, differentiated for the audience by means of the revolving scene change which momentarily shows the two spaces together *and* separate. The mechanical quality of this change on the horizontal plane is later highlighted by verbal and acoustic evidence of changes on a vertical plane, making the spatial organization of Irma's theater (and Genet's) even more complex, giving it the quality of a very complicated "theater machine":

> CARMEN (*in the wings*): Lock Studio 14! Elyane, hurry up! And *lower the studio. . . .* no, no, wait—(*we hear the sound of a rusty cap wheel, the kind made by certain old lifts*).
>
> (p. 54; my emphasis)

There is no doubt that the house contains many studios, or at least several capable of being permuted and changed to perform as many, for there is much evidence of simultaneous studio-use in the play:

> CARMEN: Stop shouting, sir. All the studios are occupied.
>
> (p. 93)

At several points in the play, Irma exultantly recites a list of her studios:

> IRMA: . . . the studio known as the Hay Studio, hung with rustic scenes, the studio of the hangings, spattered with blood and tears, the Throne-room Studio, draped in velvet with a fleur-de-lis pattern, the Studio of Mirrors, the Studio of State, the Studio of Perfumed Fountains, the Urinal Studio, the Amphitrite Studio, the Moonlight Studio. . . .
>
> (p. 37)

The variety and extension of this bill of fare are contrasted with Irma's final revelation about the spatial organization of her establishment, the significance of which is emphasized by its position in her final address to the audience. Irma's message to the spectators confirms that they have been tricked into accepting a fictional spatial organization which does not in fact exist, being as fluid and manipulable as fictional construct:

> IRMA: . . . Thirty-eight studios! Every one of them gilded, and all of them rigged with machinery so as to be able to fit into and combine with each other. . . .
>
> (p. 95)

The theme of spatial ambiguity, developed theatrically from the beginning by means of contradictory signifiers, forms the physical basis for a postmodern metaphysics. The spaces of *The Balcony* are not only theatrical and dramatic but also psychological and spiritual levels at which a similar ambiguity is achieved. They offer a challenge to the many conceptual systems which employ a topographical metaphor. These systems include: the ethical (where "good" and "evil" = "up" and "down"), the social ("belonging" vs. "exile" = "inside" vs. "outside"), the psychological ("integrated" vs. "alienated" =

"single" vs. "multiple"), and so on. The experimental spaces of *The Balcony* are all dedicated to blurring and overthrowing these topographically conceived oppositions.

For the brothel's clients, each studio is an experience of Hell, its function to obliterate guilt by providing a context of pure evil, excluding guilt by excluding any alternative to evil:

> THE BISHOP: Here there's no possibility of doing evil. *You live in evil.* In the absence of remorse. *How could you do evil?*
>
> (p. 10; my emphasis)

The moral immunity of the Balcony as Hell, as place of absolute evil, associates it with another kind of space, a social space with an equally moralistic function. In scene 2, the Judge reveals as strong a belief as the Bishop's in the Balcony's pure immorality:

> THE JUDGE: I was going to fill Hell with the souls of the damned, to fill Prisons! Prisons! Prisons, dungeons, blessed places *where evil is impossible since they are the crossroads of all the malediction in the world. One cannot commit evil in evil.*
>
> (p. 20; my emphasis)

Thus, at the level of some of the characters' experience of it, the Balcony is Hell, is a prison, not merely as the Bishop says, because it is the realm of pretense ("The Devil makes believe. That's how one recognizes him. He's the great Actor" (p. 10)), but because it is entered through a kind of "death," through denying one's *self* (that which is uniquely personal) by plunging into a *role,* which is a virtual, and consequently a *shared, conventional,* identity:

> THE JUDGE: If every judgment were delivered seriously, each one would cost me my life. That's why I'm dead. I inhabit the region of exact freedom. I, King of Hell, weight those who are dead, like me.
>
> (p. 17)

This "death" is the loss of personal identity; it is also the realm of the Same, for, being beyond life, it is also beyond difference.

As spiritual or mythic space, then, the studios are associated (again: in the experience of the clients) with Hell and with death. To enter them, they feel, is to *descend,* to burrow beneath the surface of things:

> THE GENERAL: So, in a little while, to the blare of trumpets, we shall descend—I on your back—to death and glory, for I am about to die. It is indeed a descent to the grave . . . but a formal and picturesque descent, by unexpected stairways.
>
> (p. 26)

The downward motion evoked in all three characters' experience of their studios becomes a visible, spatial fact in the last studio we see—The Mausoleum Studio—"the most beautiful of all, ultimate adornment, crown of the edifice" (p. 37). Although thus "crowning" the House of Illusions, being the "peak" of Irma's accomplishments, the Mausoleum Studio is supposedly *underground*. The epitome or prototype of all the studios (since "the scenarios are all reducible to a major theme... Death" (pp. 87–88)), this studio, quite logically, appears also to epitomize depth and descent. Its concentric structure, combined with its two stairways, gives it the appearance of a downward moving spiral, and, in its perfect form, it would be covered with soft mud into which one could "sink."

The spiritual paradigm of all the studios, most fully and concretely realized in the Mausoleum Studio, is Hell, death, and descent. The spatial axis that seems to structure this paradigm is the vertical, and movement along it, as far as the client's experience goes, is definitely downward. This direction is contrasted, however, with the direction of Mme Irma's experience, which, while still remaining on the vertical axis, moves in the opposite direction— upwards:

> IRMA: My dear, *I've succeeded in lifting it from the ground*... I unloosed it long ago, and it's flying. I cut the moorings. It's flying. Or, if you like, it's sailing in the sky, and I with it.... Darling, *the house really does take off, leaves the earth,* sails in the sky, when, in the secrecy of my heart, I call myself, but with great precision, a keeper of a bawdy house.
>
> (pp. 36–37; my emphasis)

While her clients descend into absence by playing other, absent roles, Mme Irma appears to ascend in the fulfillment of her "real" (i.e., dramatic) role. Restated in psychological terms, experience of the spaces of the brothel affords the possibility of both repression (clients) and sublimation (Irma).

This psychological duality is, in turn, a metaphor for an ideological duality, for the various characters' individual experience—which I have called spiritual and psychological—is transformed for us by a political *context* (the supposed revolution going on in the dramatic/fictional realm). This context renders the repression-sublimation opposition political, as follows: repression, descent, depth = powerlessness; sublimation, ascent, height = power. The clients' powerlessness is the obverse of Irma's power, which, as we will see, is a function of her control of *information,* her ubiquity, by means of a mechanical spying instrument, in the theatrical realm. This ideological duality occurs again at the dramatic level, where the power function is embodied no longer by Irma but by the Envoy. This character, entering the (inner) dramatic world of The Balcony from another (outer) dramatic world (the unseen world of the streets and the palace), comes to occupy a central place in the play—

indeed, he is the point at which the various worlds intersect. As such, he is also the point from which the various worlds are deconstructed. For example, the Envoy creates a fiction (of the Queen) which simultaneously gives her being *and* deprives her of it—everything the Envoy says of the Queen makes her more and more elusive; every reference to her (as a presence) makes her more and more absent. Like Irma at another level, the Envoy has knowledge which he refuses to impart fully. It is knowledge he uses (by imparting, by withholding) for creating fiction, a fiction which, like the theatrical realm created and controlled by Irma, deprives others of being, of power, and places them in a sign system of which they are the signs. As Irma controls the theatrical system, the Envoy controls the dramatic.

The various oppositions—the spatial, the psychological, the ideological—are, by virtue of the relationship between the various realms they furnish, unstable: they are false oppositions. Their terms are actually confounded and mutually erased so as also to confound the apparent opposition between real roles and fake ones. Quite appropriately, the focus of this confounded opposition is the Mausoleum Studio, supposedly dedicated to the image (i.e., the absence) of the Chief of Police, who is still "real," still present. Unlike the three clients who play the roles of (absent) Bishop, Judge, and General, and Irma, who plays the role of a (present) Madame, the Chief of Police wishes to transform his present existence into an absence—to become an image for others.

His studio embodies this contradiction in a number of ways, the first of which is a gap between its dramatic existence (verbally conveyed) and its theatrical existence. The studio seen in scene 9, and referred to as the Mausoleum Studio, *appears* to be the Chief's studio, but is—in theatrical fact—Roger's studio, bearing all the marks of this latter's fantasy pursuit. Thus the theatrical space of scene 9 represents the Chief of Police's fantasy *as distorted by Roger's fantasy,* remade, in fact, for Roger.

Roger's studio, then, is the point at which the many oppositions set up by the play are confounded and erased. His studio is described as being neither underground nor airborne, but both—it is beneath the earth's surface, yet also above it, for it is burrowed into a mountain:

> CARMEN: As you have requested, the whole mountain will be burrowed and tunnelled ... *No one will be able to see anything from the outside.* All they'll know is that *the mountain is sacred.* ...
>
> (p. 88; my emphasis)

The mountain is sacred, and (or *because*?) it is spatially mysterious, ambiguous, deceptive. It is a perfect combination of outside and inside, revealed and hidden, above and below, solid and hollow, public and private, natural and human, known and unknown. Its surface, moreover, is merely the first of many, for the space within the mountain is a space of progressive inclusion, of spaces fitted one into another:

> CARMEN: All they'll know is that the mountain is sacred, but inside, the tombs are already being enshrined in tombs, the cenotaphs in cenotaphs, the coffins in coffins, the urns...
>
> (p. 88)

The image is one of progressive and endless interiority, and this ceaseless interiority, although evoked here as part of the fiction created for Roger, is also the key to Genet's postmodern definition of the self and of human existence. For the one image so conspicuous by its absence from the play, although so persistently pursued in both poetic and theatrical terms, is the image of a *center*. The center is, by the play's definition, that which is always elsewhere, always "there," always "not-here." It is manifested only as a nostalgia for being-here-and-now, a desire which like all desires is by definition other than its object. In semiotic terms, it is the lost primary signified, approachable (but never attained) through an endless chain of signifiers which are always other than it.

Roger's Mausoleum Studio is the perfect example of this fictional, always-other center. Created in response to the Chief's wish to occupy a niche at the center of a studio of death, the studio turns out, when we see it and as the client experiences it, to be only a *part* of the poetic mausoleum described by Carmen. What Roger, as the client who has come to play the role of the Chief of Police, can experience is not the center where the Image supposedly exists, but an approach to it, a stage on the path downward and inward:

> ROGER: What about here, where I am now?
> CARMEN (*with a gesture of disdain*): An antechamber. An antechamber called the Valley of the Fallen.
>
> (p.88)

The intersection of two worlds, the theatrical (Roger) and the dramatic (the Chief), is here expanded to include another world—the historical. "The Valley of the Fallen" is, in Genet's original French text, rendered not in French but in Spanish: "Valle de los Caídos." This is, some spectators will realize, the name given by General Franco of Spain to a vast underground mausoleum he had built—using forced labor—ostensibly as a memorial to the fallen soldiers of the Spanish war, actually as a grand memorial to himself. Genet's historical reference is fleeting, deftly pulling into the play—though without any attempt to explicate or expand the allegory—a historical dimension, an ideological system which thus contextualizes the theatrical and dramatic systems being mutually opposed and undermined. This new system, the "real," takes its place in the deconstructive dialectic of the play.

Even for those spectators who miss the historical reference, Carmen's words come as a surprise. The audience, as well as the characters who have been constituted as an audience for Roger's performance, have been led to believe that what they are seeing *is* the Mausoleum Studio, not a *part* of it. And indeed, as we see Roger's experience through to the end, this space *is*, theatrically, the Mausoleum Studio, all there is of it. Thus Carmen's assurance to Roger that "In a little while, you'll go further down" (p. 88) turns out to be false, for she soon begins to hustle him away, out of his role. It is interesting to note the stage direction that Genet adds to Carmen's promise of further progress downward and inward. She makes the promise as she herself "*mounts* the underground stairway" (p. 88; my emphasis)—suggesting that Roger's experience of further interiority must be derived purely in relation to herself.

Her role in the studio thus takes on a new significance: she is not merely a *guide* come to introduce Roger to the space of his fantasy, but a crucial and significant *participant* in the fantasy, paradigmatic with the sinner (scene 1), the thief and executioner (scene 2), and the horse (scene 3). I will return to this point later.

Meanwhile, Roger does not, as he is promised, "go further down" (at least not physically; he does, however, descend "plus bas" psychologically: his abrogation of political power and responsibility is finally absolute when he castrates himself). The studio as it exists theatrically has no further depth, and its center is not the poetic center Roger seeks. Once again Genet exploits the disjunction between theatrical and dramatic, evoking a dramatic (fictional, nonexistent) center displaced by a theatrical (real, visible) center, the inner "well," which is, in dramatic terms, off-center. The "real" (i.e., fictional) center is unseen, invisible, and therefore (since "in the world of the theater, everything takes place in the visible world and nowhere else") nowhere, nonexistent.

The Mausoleum Studio, then, is Genet's theatrical sign for the process and possibility of self-realization. It seems to redefine that process as an eternal approach, without arrival, an experience of centerless interiority, of endless layers of surfaces without a core. Moreover, the relation of the Mausoleum Studio to the "dramatic" realm of the Balcony, represented by Irma's room, enhances this postmodern and theatrical definition of the self, for it too exploits the contradiction between the fictional/dramatic and theatrical levels. The Mausoleum Studio, which is supposed to be underground, is quite conspicuously positioned not *below* but *at the same level* as Irma's room; it is contiguous to it (or contained within it, another example of the T ⊂ D premise): "Then the two panels of the double mirror forming the back of the stage [and the rear wall of Irma's room] silently draw apart, revealing the interior of the Mausoleum Studio" (p. 87). The physical and dramatic relationship between Irma's room and the Mausoleum Studio (the spatial semiotics of scene 9, which I will discuss later), an ambiguous and contradictory relationship, is to the spatial semiotics of *The Balcony* what the Mausoleum Studio is to the other studios: an epitome, as well as a final, definitive statement. To understand this statement fully, it is necessary once more to return to the beginning of the play, for the relationship between Irma's Room and the Mausoleum Studio is established by a diachronic development as well as by a constant, synchronic system, revealed early in the play.

The Theatrical Paradigm of *The Balcony*

The significance of the unchanging chandelier is, as I have said, partially space-structural. Remaining constant while the rest of the décor changes, the chandelier is a sign that the play's early scenes form not a syntagm but a system, a paradigm. Scenes 1 through 3 may therefore be regarded not as different messages but as three versions of the same message, sharing the same form, the same deep structure. It is possible to study the form of this message, its structure, apart from its varied pseudocontents (I call the details of each scene pseudocontents because the real content emanates from the form: aesthetic structure has its own meaning before substance is poured into it). I propose first to describe this structure or system as it is realized in scenes 1, 2, and 3, and then to discuss its use in the rest of the play. Recalling my discussion of Genet's initial premise, T ⊂ D, I will refer to this system as the *Theatrical Paradigm*. The theatrical paradigm has three main terms, corresponding to three major theatrical subsystems: décor, actors, and costumes.

Décor

The décor of scene 1 is, as I have shown, a collection of scenic signs each of which has two levels of signification: a dramatic one and a theatrical or semiosic one. Thus "the set *seems to represent* a sacristy" (my emphasis). It is not a sacristy, i.e., not a perfectly iconic sign but one in which the difference between signifier and signified is apparent enough to make it *seem to* represent, instead of directly representing. The physical form of this difference is seen in the opposition between the three folding screens and the walls, an opposition which, Genet's stage direction implies, should be clearly visible. The set made up by the screens, and the stage space delimited by them, appear therefore as the *décor of a décor,* the second décor being defined by the walls and enclosing a larger stage space, a more "permanent" realm soon to be fully established by the chandelier. Scene 1 presents, therefore, a stage space containing a "stage" space, "real" walls surrounding pseudowalls.

These pseudowalls, the screens, are a basic element of the paradigm, and must be considered fully, synchronically and diachronically. Synchronically (i.e., in every instance of their use), the screens are signs with a single but ambiguous signified: they signify both spatial demarcation and spatial fluidity. They are boundaries, but weak, fragile ones; limits, but temporary, partial ones. They define an area of false privacy, of inadequate protection. As pseudowalls they are shorter or narrower than the "real" walls and are made of a weaker material—cloth. Thus their power of spatial definition is derived not from their material nature—i.e., it is not a "natural" power—but from an arbitrary decision to confer on their capacity for visual definition other, more substantial kinds of definition. Their function seems, therefore, to be one of virtual or ritual separation, and as such they are reminiscent of what anthropologists call the ritual "frame": "To look at itself a society must cut out a piece of itself for inspection. *To do this it must set up a frame* within which images and symbols of what has been sectioned off can be scrutinized, assessed, and, if need be, remodeled and rearranged. In ritual what is inside the frame is what is often called 'sacred', what is outside the 'profane', the 'secular', or 'mundane'. *To frame is to enclose in a border. A sacralized space has borders*" (my emphasis).[27] The screens of Genet's theatrical paradigm begin by performing this framing function, but it is not so much the ritual within as the frame itself that commands attention as the paradigm is made to participate in the drama. The play develops as a dialectic between sacred and profane, theatrical and dramatic, and its action is soon located not in the one or the other, but at the point of their intersection—in the frame itself. From the very beginning *The Balcony* is a play about boundaries, limits, lines of division. In semiotic terms, it is a play about the space between the signifier and the signified, or difference.

The drama of boundaries begins in scene 1, introduced first with visual (scenic) signs. The back screen of this scene bears two inscriptions: the crucifix drawn in trompe l'oeil, and a "built-in door." The material difference between these two signs, one "fake," the other "real," is illusory. For a door in a screen is perfectly useless: the stage space created by the screens could more easily be entered through the spaces between the screens than through one of them. Nevertheless, it is there, this door—not a fake door drawn in trompe l'oeil (a possibility to which the crucifix bears clear witness) but a real door which opens and closes.

How real, however, is this door? What does it open into, what does it close out? Nothing: virtual, ritual space. It is a real door only in that—so that—it can be opened and closed, an accessory to the ritual within, which requires complete and ostentatious privacy:

THE BISHOP: And all the doors must be closed. Firmly closed, shut, buttoned, laced, hooked sewn. . . .

(pp. 8–9)

Privacy and the invasion of it, are important aspects of the drama of boundaries, the social version of an "invasion" we will find on the psychological level. In scene 2, the client again stresses the need for complete privacy, for firm enclosure:

THE JUDGE: Are all the doors firmly shut? Can anyone see us, or hear us?

(p. 16)

The door to which the Executioner moves in response to the Judge's nervous query is a substantial door with a "huge bolt." It is also a door which can be opened a crack to peer into the next room:

THE JUDGE: May I have a look?
THE EXECUTIONER: Just a quick one, because it's getting late. (*The Executioner shrugs his shoulders and exchanges a wink with the thief.*)
THE JUDGE (*after looking*): It's lit up. Brightly lit, but empty.

(p. 16)

The executioner's conspiratorial wink to the thief has a strange effect on the information that the Judge relays to them (and us). The brilliant emptiness we cannot see is brought sharply into opposition with the sounds we have heard ("A noise is heard, as of something having fallen in the next room"): a disjunction, a difference, is introduced between two acoustic signs—the noise and the Judge's words. Once again, Genet's attack is on the traditional use of acoustic signs to designate unseen, but stable, dramatic places.

A similar exploitation of the acoustic sign occurs in the development of the offstage woman's scream which punctuates the first three scenes. In scene 1 the scream is greeted by Irma only with mild irritation:

(*Suddenly a scream of pain, uttered by a woman offstage*)
IRMA (*annoyed*): But I told them to be quiet. Good thing I remembered to cover the windows with padded curtains.

(p. 8)

The acoustic invasion seems, at this point, to be a mere in-house indiscretion, a minor flaw within the system, but still perfectly under Irma's control, easily remedied. The second time, however, Irma's confidence in her power to create the required illusion of secrecy ("They're at it again! I'll go and shut them up") is shaken by the client's disturbing reading of the sign:

THE BISHOP: That wasn't a make-believe scream.
IRMA (*anxiously*): I don't know ... Who knows and what does it matter?

(p. 11)

Actually, it matters a great deal. The nature of the scream (theatrical or dramatic, make-believe or "real") is linked to the question of the house's impregnability. The privacy so dear to the clients is equally precious to Irma: the theatrical paradigm mirrors the dramatic one:

IRMA: One thing we mustn't forget—if we ever get out of this mess—is that the walls aren't sufficiently padded and the windows aren't well sealed ... *One can hear what's going on in the street. Which means that from the street one can hear what's going on in the house.*

(p. 34; my emphasis)

This *mutual* acoustic invasion of public and private spaces—a symbol, as I will show later, of the vulnerability of the self—is pervasive. Even at the end, even in the most profound and complex interiority of the Mausoleum Studio, this invasion of the secret and sacred by the mundane and profane cannot be prevented:[28]

(*Suddenly, the sound of a hammer striking an anvil. Then a cock crows*)
ROGER: Is life so near?
CARMEN (*in a normal voice, not acting*): As I've told you, everything's padded, but some sounds always manage to filter through ... you must stop listening to the sounds from the outside.

(pp. 89–90)

While correct utilization of the theatrical paradigm (the studios) seems to require an active disregard of contradictory acoustic evidence, there is another kind of spatial violation that is even harder to resolve. We have seen that the client's desire is for *complete* privacy ("Can anyone see us, *or hear us?*"). Indeed, secrecy seems to be a central element of the rituals Mme Irma has contracted to provide:

IRMA: In any case, even if it were celebrated here, I wouldn't see anything. The ceremonies are secret.

(p. 48)

As the chief's retort immediately reveals, this essential secrecy is altogether fake:

THE CHIEF OF POLICE: You liar. You've got secret peep-holes in every wall. Every partition, every mirror is rigged. In one place, you can hear the sighs, in another the echo of the moans. . . .

(p. 48)

The chief's accusation is supported by the presence, on stage, of a concrete sign of this visual violation of private space. Irma's room contains *"an apparatus by means of which Irma can see what is going on in the studios"* (p. 29). It is not simply a matter of occasional or whimsical eavesdropping as the Bishop suggests at one point; the presence of the apparatus asserts that some sort of covert surveillance is *essential* to the running and coordination of The Balcony's intricate and fluid spaces. Thus contradiction resides at the heart of the paradigm: the illusion of privacy depends upon constant and reliable intrusion, upon institutionalized *violation* of that privacy.[29]

It is not hard to detect an allusion, in this, to the functioning of the theatrical "machine," especially as it operates in the case of realistic theater. The so-called fourth wall is, by its absence-presence, the mark of a simultaneous separation and continuity, of a private world that is public. The constituting paradox of realistic drama is that what is essentially there *to be seen* (a play) is structured around the (false) premise that it *cannot be seen*.

This paradox is duplicated in *The Balcony* at the dramatic level, for the brothel's own precious isolation is first threatened *visually*:

> IRMA: See to it she doesn't scream so loud. *The house is being watched.*
>
> (p. 43; my emphasis)

It is not long before the threat posed by this visual intrusion is more concretely fulfilled. When the rebellion, at first only heard (/machine-gun fire/), spoken about, feared, finally erupts into the drama, its immediate effect is seen at the level of *boundaries*—in this case, the walls of the brothel. Entering first as a fatal bullet that shatters a windowpane (the weakest part of the room's limits), it then goes on to redefine those limits altogether, transforming the solid surface of exclusion into a kind of broken lacework that makes the outside a part of the inside:

> IRMA: ... The populace is howling beneath my windows, which have been multiplied by the bombs.
>
> (p. 63)

Once again, the definitive theatrical statement of spatial intrusion occurs in scene 9, where the stage expands to include both the site of surveillance and the space surveyed. As the characters in Irma's room take their positions at the viewing mechanism to witness Roger's Mausoleum ritual, a hierarchy of spaces and visual modes is put into operation: the audience watches the characters watching Roger. It is another version of the expanded premise Theatrical^1 $\subset$ Dramatic $\subset$ Theatrical^2, which is now specified to read as follows:

> *Actors*[1] are watched by *Actors*[2] are watched by *Audience*
> (Roger-Carmen)   (Irma and company)

or

> *Actors* are watched by *Audience*[1] are watched by *Audience*[2]
> (Roger-Carmen)   (Irma and company)

The ambiguity of the position of the central term (the dramatic group, who are both Actors[2] and Audience[1]) once again spreads in both directions, destabilizing or relativizing the roles of both actors and spectators by introducing an element of reciprocity between them. This reciprocity is heightened by the strong reflexive nature of Roger's ritual: he (indeed, all the clients) requires the participation of *viewers* to realize his fantasy role: the roles are fulfilled when they are *seen,* acknowledged by someone else, or, in semiotic terms, stand *for something to somebody*:

> ROGER: So your glory accompanies mine? (To Carmen) Does he mean that my reputation will be kept going by his words? And ... if he says nothing I'll cease to exist...?
>
> (p. 90)

and later:

> THE SLAVE (*with exaltation*): ... You're so splendid: so splendid that I wonder whether you're aglow or whether you're all the darkness of all the nights?
> ROGER: What does it matter, since I'm no longer to have any reality except in the reality of your phrases?
>
> (p. 91)

In the ritual of self-realization provided by the Balcony's theatrical paradigm, to be is to be perceived. To become one's self is to absent oneself from direct personal experience and to become objectified—an image, a song, a *sign—for others*. And this "objective imperative" is, as the spatial hierarchy of scene 9 dramatizes, also quintessentially theatrical.

The spaces and spatial relationships of scene 9, which replicate the spaces and spatial relationships of theater (both involve an opposition of two spaces that are simultaneously contiguous and disjunct, linked by a one-way mechanism of perception), have one other interesting feature: the boundary that initially separates them is a *mirror*: "*a large two-panelled mirror ... forms the* [rear] *wall*" (p. 70). The "inner space" of scene 9, which is revealed when the rear mirror panel parts, can be conceived, figuratively, as what was "in the mirror," or the mirror image. This would imply a relationship of identity (or reflection) between Mme Irma's room and the Mausoleum Studio (although the identity would not, of course, be literal but only metaphorical, for the two spaces are literally *separate*, though contiguous). The meaning of this implication emerges in the context of the many and varied uses of mirrors and mirror images in the play, which form a sort of subparadigm within the theatrical paradigm.

The mirrors. The décor of scene 1 includes a sign which falls somewhere in between the chandelier and the screens on the theatrical-dramatic continuum. While the chandelier is always quite literally "the same" (it does not move at all), and while the screens are structurally permanent (recurring in scenes 1/2/3) but substantially different (each set of screens is a new one, bearing a different inscription: crucifix, door, color), the mirror is both structurally and materially—but not literally—the same. Since it is attached to one of the *walls* (not to one of the screens), which moves out of sight when the stage revolves to change the scene, the mirror is, at its first level of signification, a sign itself that the "real" walls (hitherto opposed to the pseudowalls of the screens) are not so "real" after all, but part of the second theatrical realm which contains the dramatic one. This signification emerges during the first scene-change, as does the semiosic signification of the chandelier. However, while the chandelier remains in view, the mirror temporarily disappears. In scene 2 it reappears, or rather, its position is occupied by another mirror exactly like it—its mirror image! The ambiguity of this sign is therefore profound, and has a profound influence on the sense of illocality that pervades the theatrical paradigm.

Besides its structural ambiguity, the mirror sign (in all three appearances) has another kind of ambiguity: its initial content is illogical, defying the laws of reflection and perception: "*On the right wall, a mirror, with a carved gilt frame, reflects an unmade bed which, if the room were arranged logically, would be in the first rows of the orchestra*" (p. 7). No doubt this arrangement is partially a symbolic statement of the audience's participation in the rituals of the brothel, a link in the chain that draws the spectators into the drama. But it is much more. It is an example of the rupture—or difference—between signifier and signified, between visible and invisible, present and absent. For what this sign stands for («a bed in the orchestra») does not exist. It is, consequently, a signifier with a signified that has no referent in reality. The surface of the mirror is therefore not a reproductive surface but a distortive one: it is a surface not of revelation but of fabrication, not of truth but of lies. As such it is a semiotic or significative system, for, to quote Eco, "*semiotics is in principle the discipline that studies everything which can be used in order to lie.*"[30] The astonishing thing here is that the semiotic/lying surface is precisely the one most frequently used by the characters (as by human beings) *to see themselves "as they really are"*: the mirror. To semiotize the mirror is to disturb the ontological and epistemological foundations of human psychology: it is to redefine the notions of "being" and of "self," or, at least, of "self-knowledge."

Let us see how this mirror is used and how it is developed. In scene 1, the mirror is used to fulfill the objective imperative in the Bishop's ritual. It is directly addressed, as if it were another character, an independent being. Yet this powerful otherness is contingent on the self, involved in a reciprocity that situates the desired experience of pure selfhood not within the self, nor within the reflection, but in between, traversing the boundary of the mirror's surface: "Do I make myself clear, mirror, gilded image?" (p. 12) asks the Bishop of his reflection. Self-realization is process, not product; success in "clarifying" oneself is a continual, unending projection outward and perception inward. The self occupies a liminal space, neither *here* nor *there,* but streaming in between them, in the effort to reconcile inside and outside, being and being perceived, subject and object. And, since the boundary it traverses is, as we have seen, a semiotic (or semiot*izing*) system, a distorting fabric, being is a type of "coding," and the self is a sign.

The mirror sustains its first structural transformation in scene 4, the logic of which derives from its relation to the paradigm already elaborated in the preceding three scenes. Scene 4 detaches itself from the paradigm by its method of appearance (it is not a part of the revolving syntagm), and by its apparent nonuse of the theatrical-dramatic dichotomy (the chandelier is absent). It seems to be pure, transcendent theater, liberated from the destabilizing reminders of dramatic context, the climax and perfection of the studio paradigm. This perfection (which promises, finally, a real fulfillment of self—i.e., total self-erasure, uninhibited and undistracted by a "real" invading context) is reflected by certain changes in the décor. Whereas the décor of the other studios contained three signifiers (/walls/, /screens/, /mirrors/) for the single signified //boundaries//, this décor collapses all three into a single element: the stage space here is enclosed by three *panels* (neither walls nor screens but something in between) which *"are three mirrors"* (p. 27) (the panels do not bear mirrors but *are,* in their entirety, mirrors). The earlier disjunction between theatrical and dramatic is here replaced by a congruence of the two, giving this scene the appearance of an independent dramatic/theatrical space, free of all the disturbance, ambiguity, and fragility found in the paradigm. Even language, which, in the preceding scenes, had shattered the sacredness of the ritual by its tendency to pull the action away from the studio and towards the fictional/dramatic rebellion outside, seems to be absent here. Mirrors, privacy, and silence—the zero signs of three systems (décor, actors, and dialogue) of the theatrical paradigm—these seem to be the requisites for a completed ritual, for a realization of the self, for a moment of genuine self-perception (the tramp even removes his glasses, hiding them first in a case and then in his pocket, as if interring within himself the visual mechanism through which the stream of the self, between subject and reflection, can flow).

The promise of fulfillment turns out, however, to be a false one. Before long the apparently solid surface of the mirrors (the zero sign of the décor system) turns out to conceal a door, revealing its participation in the system of the theatrical paradigm, where the décor is a matter of weak boundaries and vulnerable spaces. Through this door the temporarily suppressed dramatic realm, which has threatened each preceding ritual with profane intrusion, enters. The silence (the zero sign of the sound and speech systems) is broken by the three raps on the door and then by the girl's answering "Yes" (p. 28). The scene ends, not with a completion of the ritual, but—like all the other scenes—with the process of self-erasure struggling against and thwarted by language, by questions and by uncertainty:

THE MAN: What about the lice?
THE GIRL (*very coarsely*): They're there.

(p. 28)

It is at this point that the crucial feature of the theatrical paradigm finally becomes apparent. Mme Irma's studios, it would seem, offer not absence from the self, not escape into a center of pure otherness, but an experience of "in-between-ness," of the *process* of self-loss. They do not provide the product itself (just as they do not provide a "center"), merely the *opportunity to experience* its impossibility. The definition of selfhood they exemplify is that of self as subject/object, as duality, as a constant traversing of boundaries.

Nor is this a "failure" of the system or the ritual. The clients' reactions (clearest in the Tramp, whose face lights up with tenderness), as well as their later negative experiences of the self as product, suggest that this "dynamic" experience of selfhood *is* the most authentic, desirable, and joyful one, the one for which they have paid.

This definition, with its accompanying paradoxes, receives its fullest theatrical statement in a feature of scene 4 I have not yet discussed: the *nature* of the all-important mirrors in the scene. I have been discussing this décor so far as if these were real mirrors with which we are dealing. In fact, they are not: the mirrors in question are—and have to be—fake: mirror illusions. A stage made up of real mirrors would reflect part of the audience in the auditorium. Now, whereas, as we have already seen, Genet frequently draws the audience into the drama, here he draws them in paradoxically, by excluding them. The mirrors are actually empty frames, each containing an actor playing *the role* of a reflection of the tramp. The audience seeks its own reflection in vain, and must finally accept as its reflection the pseudoreflections of the tramp. The trick mirrors of the early scenes had constituted the auditorium space as a brothel space; the fake mirrors of this scene constitute each spectator as a mangy masochist paying to be whipped. The audience's experience of the play, like the clients' experience of their roles, thus becomes process, streaming between two spaces and traversing the weak boundary of the so-called fourth wall. Once again, being is neither here nor there, but in between, liminal.

This experience is largely a function of the *subverting* of the mirror sign by the substitution of actors for reflections. A mirror reflection is, as I have said, not a sign, not part of a communication act. Another way of putting this is that it is a *defeat* of semiosis, a "communication" that does not communicate, for it collapses together various elements of the communication model: "source and addressee coincide...; receiver and transmitter coincide; expression and content coincide since the content of the reflected image is just the image of a body, not the body itself."[31] Genet's treatment of the mirror vanquishes its nonsemiosic quality, reintroducing semiosis into the act of self-perception.

A final use of the mirror sign occurs in scene 9, which is, as I have said before, both the perfection and the destruction of the theatrical paradigm. The dramatic place represented in scene 9 is Mme Irma's room, but as theatrical space it differs in one important respect from its earlier aspect in scene 5. Whereas the first set for this place was dominated by lace ("Large lace hangings suspended from the flies" (p. 78))—a material whose semiotic role I will discuss later—the set of scene 9 exchanges those lace hangings for "a large two-panelled mirror which forms the [rear] wall" (p. 70). As before, the relationship between this place and the studios is ambiguous. In scene 5, that relationship was signified by the presence of "the same chandelier" and, perhaps more intriguingly, by the statement that "It is the same room that was reflected in the mirror in the first three scenes." Those mirrors, we recall, bore the reflection of an unmade bed which appeared to be located *in the first rows of the auditorium*. The appearance of this bed in scene 5 establishes the following equation: Mme Irma's Room = Auditorium. It is this equation which is developed in scene 9, where the rear mirror parts to reveal the quintessential Mausoleum Studio, and by doing so constitutes the actors in Irma's room as a kind of second-order audience, looking at and looked at, watching and being watched. The model of theatrical experience thus created is analogous to the model of self-realization I have discussed. To be is both to perceive and to *be* perceived, or, more accurately, it is to perceive being perceived, a dual requirement which contains the germ of impossibility, for it defines both theatricality and self-realization as an endless and circular process.

The essential reciprocity between Roger and the slave is further complicated by the fact that the slave is "the character seen in scene four" (p.

89). In short, what scene 9 provides is an example, at the level of character/role, of the combinative or transformational nature of theater which the Mausoleum Studio provides at the level of space. "... The scenarios are all reducible to a major theme ... death"; are the participants all reducible to a major role: the slave's? The tramp, who had appeared to be a client in scene 4, appears now to be an actor provided by the establishment to realize Roger's fantasy. This transformation in his status clears the way for an appraisal of the second element of the paradigm: actors.

Actors

An actor in a role constitutes a sign in which the physical human being is the signifier and the character is the signified. In *The Balcony* this sign is, like others, presented in rupture, its semiotic nature revealed by insistence on its dual and disjunct character. The slave/tramp character, an instance of one signifier with two successive signifieds, foregrounds the difference inherent in the actor sign. Why, we might ask, does Genet specifically require the roles of the tramp and the slave to be played by the same actor? What particular meaning, problem, effect, or solution does this authorial demand create? Conversely, what significant element of the play would be forfeited by a production that ignores this demand?

The answers to these questions must be sought within the semiotic theme and the post-modern, performative mode of the play, for the dual-role phenomenon is one that becomes significant only in performance. Indeed, any performance that follows Genet's requirement without also *manifesting* it (that is, without making it clear to the audience that this is in fact the same *actor* they have previously encountered in another guise) would actually be failing the T-Text on this point. The question therefore becomes, what is achieved by making the audience realize that the role of slave is being played by the actor who played the tramp?

One possible, and initial, message might be that the *character* Tramp is playing a part in the Mausoleum version of the studio paradigm. The implication then would be that Mme Irma's creative genius and business acumen have found a way to service two clients at once while at the same time reducing the number of brothel personnel in her employ. This solution, simple though it may seem, is soon found to have implications that prompt a review of the earlier studio scenes.

If the client who wished to play a tramp can later play slave to Roger's Chief of Police, might not those actors seen earlier playing sinner, thief, executioner, and horse be clients similarly playing opposite other clients? Might not Mme Irma's establishment be, in fact, a space of total fantasy and role-playing, in which not one character is what he or she appears to be, but rather a character (of unknown identity) playing a role?

The destabilization of identity resulting from such a line of reasoning is hinted at several times in the play. The characer of Arthur is perhaps the most obvious case of fluid identity. When first seen, this actor is dressed as an executioner, although the theatrical context makes it clear that he is not a "real" executioner but a brothel employee playing an executioner for the "Judge's" benefit. The Arthur sign, in other words, is already in the process of unravelling. Furthermore, Arthur's function in scene 2 requires that this sign sustain a series of ruptures, corresponding to the series of stages through which the Judge's fantasy moves. At first, he is merely a representative of the establishment, with the task of reassuring the client about the secrecy of the anticipated ritual:

> THE JUDGE: Are all the doors firmly shut? Can anyone see us, or hear us?
> THE EXECUTIONER: No, no, you needn't worry. I bolted the door....
> THE JUDGE: Are you sure?
> THE EXECUTIONER: You can take my word for it.
>
> (p. 16)

From ritual assistant Arthur moves toward his role of ritual participant, playing brutal executioner to the client's judge:

> THE EXECUTIONER: Shall I let her have it? Shall I, my Lord?
>
> (p. 18)

En route to this role he has taken a detour into the spiritual space occupied by the Judge, playing Cerberus to the Judge's King of Hell:

> THE JUDGE: ... In the depths of Hell I sort out the humans who venture there. (*To the Executioner*) Cerberus?
> THE EXECUTIONER (*imitating the dog*): Bow-wow, Bow-wow!
> THE JUDGE: You're handsome! And the sight of a fresh victim makes you even handsomer. (*He curls up the Executioner's lips*) Show your fangs. Dreadful. White.
>
> (pp. 17–18).

Arthur's final role in this scene, and his most important, involves that reciprocity of being that defines selfhood in the play. It is as the image or reflection of the Judge that the Arthur sign culminates, fulfilling the ritual demand for total self-erasure:

> THE JUDGE (*He pretends to look at himself in the Executioner.*): Mirror that glorifies me! Imagine that I can touch, I love you... *Are you there?* You're all there, my huge arm, too heavy for me, too big, too fat for my shoulder, walking at my side all by myself! Arm, hundredweight of meat, *without you I'd be nothing.*
>
> (pp. 18-19; my emphasis)

The contingent nature of personal identity is axiomatic in *The Balcony*. It exists between Roger and the Slave, between the Judge and the Executioner. It is something everyone in Mme Irma's establishment understands, although its most eloquent realization belongs to a client:

> THE JUDGE (*to the Thief*): My being a judge is an emanation of your being a thief. You need only refuse—but you'd better not!—need only refuse to be who you are—what you are, therefore, who you are—for me to cease to be...to vanish, evaporated. Burst. Volatilized. Denied.
>
> (p. 19)

The other side of this being-in-others is non-being-in-self, and once again it is Arthur who exemplifies this. Having seen him as an Executioner, as Cerberus, as mirror image, we see him next in another role, that of Pimp to Irma's Madame. In scene 5, Arthur appears in *"classical pimp's outfit: light grey suit, white felt hat, etc."* (p. 42). That this attire is a costume, the dress of a role rather than of a person, is quickly established:

> CARMEN: And in any case, Mr. Arthur, you're wearing an outfit that doesn't allow you to joke. The pimp has a grin, never a smile.
>
> IRMA: She's right.
>
> (p. 43)

Once again, the signifier (the costume/role) floods the signified (the character/person), obscuring it to the point of nonexistence. Through all his guises, Arthur remains absent, a purely perceptual object with no substance, a surface even when used sexually. He is "a pillar, a shaft, a phallus" (p. 53), says Irma, which makes him, paradoxically, a woman: "I'm his man and he relies on me, but I need that rugged shop-window dummy hanging on to my skirts. He's my body," she concludes in words reminiscent of the Judge's, "but set beside me" (p. 53). It is perfectly appropriate that it is Arthur who plays the corpse in this play, condensing in that role the many instances of absence that have made up his theatricality:

> IRMA: He's no man, he's my stage-prop.
>
> (p. 39)

It is as stage-props, as objects, paradoxically, that Genet's people exist. The movement towards subjectivity is a movement of objectification, and self is discovered as it struggles to disappear, to attain absence.

The postmodern self defined in *The Balcony* is, like avant-garde theater, a process rather than a product, a becoming rather than a being. It is a dynamic forever threatened by stasis, an experience of movement and anticipation always in danger of paralysis. Its antithesis exists in the play as the grotesque enterprise of the three photographers (more machines than humans themselves as they stand behind their tripods with their heads draped in black). Once revealed, as it is in the play, their creation—"A true image, born of a false spectacle" (p. 75)—destroys not only itself but also, by analogy, the dramatic reality of the play's characters (i.e., their "role"-existence). The newly realized Bishop, Judge, and General are, in their experience as well as ours, as unreal as the fake images registered by the photographers. Each man laments his lost fantasy, defantasized and denatured by immobility. Once realized, the roles of Bishop, General, and Judge lose their power of self-realization. Arrested, movement evaporates, coagulates into the stasis of nonexperience:

> THE GENERAL: At no moment can I prepare myself—I used to start a month in advance—prepare myself for pulling on my general's boots and breeches. I'm rigged in them for all eternity. By Jove, I no longer dream.
> THE JUDGE: I'm just a dignity represented by a skirt.
>
> (p. 80)

By a strange twist, the equivalence of signifier and signified described by the Judge brings not satisfaction but disappointment and constraint. It traps the self in a rigid joyless correspondence of role and experience, precluding the anticipation, imagination, and potentiality required by the self-as-process.

My discussion of Genet's postmodern definition of selfhood has stressed the uniquely theatrical terms of that definition, and it is Genet's ability to align the philosophical with the theatrical that I wish to emphasize. In arguing for a conception of selfhood as process, Genet also argues for a theatrical vision of theater, a vision of theater as presence and as process. Translated into theatrical terms, the semiotic stasis decried by the realized judge amounts to a return to mimetic dramaturgy, in which the actor is trapped within the character, permanently located in an otherness which, affording no escape, also affords no experience. The rigid equivalence of signifier and signified, of actor and character, is a denial of difference. It eradicates that terrifying abyss between self and other which is the only space of self-realization. For Genet, theatricality inhabits the liminal space and time of conscious make-believe, that moment when, to use his example, the elevated host is neither bread nor flesh but a potentiality born of the spiritual yearnings of the congregation. The experience of theater, as well as the experience of self, resides in the vast space of nothing between desire and its fulfillment, self and other, actor and character, signifier and signified. The denial of this powerful space, this "*difference,*" transforms experience into slavery:

> THE BISHOP: So long as we were in a room in a brothel, we belonged to our own fantasies. But once having exposed them, having named them, having proclaimed them, we're now tied up with human beings, tied to you, and forced to go on with this adventure according to the law of visibility.
>
> (p. 79)

The laws of visibility govern the dead world of equivalence, where people are their roles and actors are their characters. In the living world of theatrical process, these laws are powerless. In this world, the relationship between signifier and signified is free, capable of incredible creativity and transformation. In this world becoming is limitless, and experience far beyond the bounds of possibility. Carmen's memory of her experience of self in the role of Madonna is a case in point:

> CARMEN: My blue veil, my blue robe, my blue apron, my blue eyes....
> IRMA: They're hazel.
> CARMEN: They were blue that day.
>
> (p. 38)

Nor is Carmen alone in knowing the self as a penetrating surface; the Bishop too experiences himself, in the play's very first moments, as the paradox of an internalized exteriority: "Mitre, bishop's bonnet, when my eyes close for the last time, it is you that I shall see behind my eyelids, you, my beautiful gilded hat...." (p. 7). It is not surprising that the terms of self-realization are theatrical (costume) and spatial (external-internal). The self, like the stage, is a space of paradox, centerless and liminal. It exists not within the body but on it, as an endlessly traversed boundary. Accordingly, an original, special significance is attached to yet another basic theatrical sign system: costumes.

Costumes

The theatrical paradigm constitutes costume not as disguise but as revelation. Garments have the power not only of penetrating into the experience of the wearer but also of drawing that experience out and transforming it. To the Bishop, his sacred garb becomes the vehicle of self-realization beyond the bounds of physicality. The body drowns in the folds of rich fabric, to surface as something else, experienced as never before:

> THE BISHOP: Ornaments! Mitres! Laces! You above all, oh gilded cope, you protect me from the world. Where are my legs, where are my arms? Under your scalloped, lustrous flaps, what have my hands been doing? Fit only for fluttering gestures, they've become stumps of wings—not of angels, but of partridges!—rigid cope...Would my hand emerge at times, knife-like, to bless? Or cut, mow down? My hand, the head of a turtle, would push aside the flaps...And go back into the rock. Underneath, my hand would dream...Ornaments, gilded copes....
>
> (p. 13)

Like space, costume is experienced as paradox and dynamic. The play even provides an emblem of this experience of costume. That emblem is lace, which bears the same relation to the play's costume system as the balcony does to its spatial system. Both are liminal, both ambiguous. Just as the balcony occupies a space at the intersection of every spatial axis, so also lace contains and negates all the properties of a garment. It covers and exposes, hides and reveals. It is a kind of material writing, inscribing the body with the message of a costume:

> THE BISHOP: Oh laces, laces, fashioned by a thousand little hands to veil ever so many panting bosoms, buxom bosoms, and faces, and hair, *you illustrate me* with branches and flowers!
>
> (p. 11; my emphasis)

I have pointed out, in my discussion of the play's spatial semiotic, the crucial role of invasion. The balcony's secret spaces are constantly being invaded—acoustically, mechanically, visually, verbally. The fragile privacy of the studios is a characteristic also of the brothel itself, which is invaded first acoustically (sounds of machine-gun fire) and then physically, as bullets enter and smash mirrors. As the play progresses, the walls of the brothel become less and less solid:

> IRMA: The populace is howling beneath my windows, which have been multiplied by the bombs.
>
> (p. 63)

The wall has become as lace, a mere trace of separation, a totally ineffectual barrier between inside and outside.

The invasion of space and the eradication of territorial boundaries, constitute the spatial "plot" or "action" of *The Balcony*. Its psychological counterpart is the experience of self as a movement between the body and its image across the surface of costume.

Deconstructing the Real

There remains a final boundary to be eradicated in order to complete the play's processive identity: the boundary between the play and its audience. This audience has, we have seen, been drawn into the play several times. In its last moments, the play moves out to constitute the audience as spectacle, as perceiving/perceived entity:

IRMA: You must go home, where everything—you can be quite sure—will be falser than here... You must go now. You'll leave by the right, through the alley.... It's morning already. (*A burst of machine-gun fire.*)

(p. 96)

The play's end denies closure. Irma speaks of preparing for the next night—a final use of the semiotic theme, since the next night is also the next performance of the play. The alley through which she instructs the audience to leave is the same through which her clients habitually make their escape, in secrecy and shame, and the homes to which she returns the audience are located in the continuum of unreality her establishment occupies. To the original formula of theatrical^1 $\subset$ dramatic $\subset$ theatrical^2 another term is now added: theatrical^1 $\subset$ dramatic $\subset$ theatrical^2 $\subset$ real. The new term, however, is explicitly redefined: the "real" world of the audience is "falser" than Irma's world, bringing it into a position of contingency vis-à-vis the spectacle they have just witnessed. It is not the dramatic which is contained within the real, therefore, but the real which is contained within the dramatic, and hence rendered fictional: real $\subset$ theatrical^1 $\subset$ dramatic $\subset$ theatrical^2. *The Balcony* is a drama of signifiers which ends by semiotizing the real. Here it is not a mirror that art holds up to life, but a sign.[32]

4

The Blacks

The ultimate gesture is performed off-stage.

Genet, *The Blacks*

No "gesture" can, semiotically speaking, be "performed off-stage." The notion of such a performance, although an old and venerable one, firmly established in classical drama and theory as a rule of dramatic "decorum," is profoundly paradoxical. When articulated within the context of a performance and incorporated into a dramatic action, the paradox is not only revealed but rendered productive in the metasemiotic code I have associated with avant-garde theater. Taken as the constitutive notion of a play—as it is in Genet's *The Blacks*—the paradox of the offstage performance organizes a semiosic drama, a drama of dramatic codes. It also functions as a tunnel of escape out of the eternal derealized regress characteristic of metatheater and into a realm of "real"—i.e., apparently "uncoded"—reality. *The Blacks* moves—*through* a metatheatrical analysis of dramatic codes—*to* a social confrontation that is ultimately unmediated by theater.

It is only in a *social,* not a *theatrical,* context that an "offstage performance" makes sense. In ordinary (that is, social) parlance, the word "performance" can refer to any action carried out by an agent: a surgeon performs an operation, a priest performs a marriage. Thus, in the *dramatic* (i.e., fictional) context, it is possible to conceive of an action being "performed" elsewhere. When, however, the context is a theatrical one, and elsewhere is "offstage," a far more restricted definition of the word performance comes into play.

In the theater, a performance is, by definition, an action that occurs *on stage* (or, more precisely, within the evidential boundaries of the spectators), an action that is capable of being *directly* perceived—visually or aurally—by the audience. (Note that this definition takes "stage" in a semiotic, not merely physical, sense, to include the "acoustic (off)stage.") Thus, if the audience "hears" the gesture (a /scream offstage/ can be an acoustic sign for //murder//), it can conclude that "a gesture has been performed offstage."

But if the so-called gesture is *truly* offstage—i.e., if it is neither seen nor heard by the audience—it cannot be said to have been "performed" at all (nor is it a "gesture" in the theatrical sense). It is clear from the handling of the above-mentioned "ultimate gesture" in *The Blacks* that this is precisely the distinction that Genet is dramatizing, for its nonexistence is clearly acknowledged:

ARCHIBALD: Is it over? Did you have much trouble?

VILLAGE: Same is usual.

SNOW: Nothing happened, did it?

VILLAGE: No, nothing. Or, if you prefer, it all went off as usual, and very smoothly. When Diouf entered behind the screen, he kindly offered me a seat.

SNOW: And then?

NEWPORT NEWS: Nothing else. They waited on a bench, off stage, and smiled at each other in amusement.[1]

What, then, can we make of so-called "offstage" events, of, for instance, the hundreds of corpses with which the stages of classical drama were decorously not strewn? The answer lies in the dual nature of the dramatic code, which includes the possibility of what *appears to be* a violation of its performance rule. This apparent violation takes the form of a subcode switch: in the case of an offstage death, the sign for "death" is coded not in a mimetic code but in a diegetic[2] one, the latter being incorporated into the former. In its capacity to move imperceptibly back and forth between the modes of mimesis and diegesis lies the drama's unique character, as well as, from a theoretical point of view, its unique problem. The constant code-switching of dramatic messages reflects the existence, in plays, of a complex ontological system, one in which several levels of existence, several types of "realities" or "worlds," are brought into relationship with each other. The relationships are made possible and meaningful by means of an underlying set of rules, known to both performers and spectators. This set of rules is the *dramatic code*.

In *The Blacks*, Genet's analysis of the dramatic code makes the play a fine example of the relationship of drama to philosophical considerations of the concept of reality. The question of reality, when asked phenomenologically, that is, the question of *our sense* of the *realness* of reality, leads to a concept that has proved to be of primary importance in the work of social scientists like Erving Goffman and Gregory Bateson. This is the concept of multiple realities, upon which the theory of meaningful social action is predicated. Experiential reality, so the argument goes, is not single but multiple: there are many "realities," also called "orders of existence" or "subuniverses," each of which "has its own special and separate style of existence."[3] It is possible for us to speak, therefore, of a physical reality, a fictional reality, a mythical reality, a dream reality, a psychotic reality, a philosophical reality (or "world of abstract and philosophical truths"),[4] and so on.

Dramatic reality, that is, that realm or order of existence governed by the dramatic code, differs from all other realities in its capacity for *containment*. On the one hand, it is itself part of other "worlds," notably the social world, for no dramatic reality can sustain itself (i.e., maintain a quality of realness) outside a social realm capable of endowing it, and willing to endow it, with meaning. This dependence on social or cultural reality is a feature of all drama, even the most unreal or "absurd"; for "it is precisely as deviations from actual-world laws whose very violation underlines their indispensability that the devices of absurdist drama are perceived. Avant-garde suspension of the cultural and ontological principles of W_0 (the actual world) may cause us to reflect on our understanding of our own world but do not break with it entirely."[5] In respect to its relationship of dependence on the social or everyday world the drama differs from other patently "unreal" or counterfactual worlds. The worlds of dream and of psychosis, for instance, require no external sanction or reference to gain their quality of realness.

On the other hand, the dramatic world is made up of—or *contains*— some portions of the very worlds that at one level constitute it and, at another, are distinguished from it. Thus Strindberg's *A Dream Play*, which is *not* a dream, contains within it a dream world. Cocteau's *The Infernal Machine* contains a mythic world; Shakespeare's *Henry V* contains a historical world; Chekhov's *The Cherry Orchard* contains a social world; and so on. In fact, the dramatic world can contain any other world, or rather, a "staged" version of any other world (including, as in metatheater, a "staged" stage world). In semiotic terms, this feature can be stated as follows: the dramatic code is a special social code which can incorporate, as subcodes, all social codes.

The matter is, of course, more complicated. For, in the process of coopting extradramatic codes, the drama transforms them, producing an effect of "derealization." The clearest example of this transformation is in the area of language. It has been noticed[6] that stage speech is inherently distanced—the fact of being spoken on stage gives it the appearance of being unreal, within "quotation marks," for it is never the utterance of the speaker but of the character this speaker represents. The "emitter" of the speech exists at a (cognitive) distance from the "intender" of the speech: the two occupy, in fact, different "worlds," one actual, the other fictional. This fact puts the study of dramatic discourse in a special area, outside the realm of normal language with which it shares all appearances. Thus the theory of speech acts, for instance, begins by carefully excluding dramatic speech from its area of inquiry: "... a performatic utterance will, for example, be *in a peculiar way* hollow or void if said by an actor on the stage.... Language in such circumstances is in special ways—intelligibly—used not seriously, but in ways *parasitic* upon its normal use—ways which fall under the doctrine of the *etiolations* of language. All this we are *excluding* from consideration" (emphasis in original).[7] In spite of being thus carefully excluded from speech act theory, the drama does not (and this is an example of the "containment" feature mentioned earlier) exclude speech acts from itself: hence it is possible to apply speech act concepts, such as illocution and perlocution, to drama,[8] so long as care is taken to distinguish between the performance and the fiction performed, for only in the latter can the theory be directly applied.

While the linguistic code provides the clearest example of the drama's tendency to recode social codes (transform them), the same principle applies to all other codes as well. Indeed the tendency is so pervasive as to be identifiable as a permanent and essential rule of the dramatic code: the semiotization principle. Not only does the theater transform nontheatrical codes like language (as well as costume, gesture, movement, etc.), it also codifies—or *semiotizes*—noncoded or "natural" phenomena. Thus any strip of behavior normally considered to be "free" or spontaneous, occurring without the benefit of a socially determined convention—such as a scream of pain emitted upon sudden contact with fire—becomes, once "scripted" to be "performed" on stage, part of a behavioral code that links the behavior not to the actual experience of the actor but to the fictional experience of the character.

The Blacks provides an interesting example of this semiotization principle, incorporating it at an early stage so as to establish the play's status as "coded" as opposed to "free." The very first words of the play (interesting in themselves in being the exact formula for "performance openers"—more on this later), "Ladies and Gentlemen," are greeted by a response of laughter by the stage audience (the Court) (p. 9). Laughter is, of course, usually thought of as a "natural" occurrence (being, in *itself,* a univeral, as opposed to a cultural, response). What is not natural—i.e., what is semiotic—about laughter is not its existence but its *manner* (i.e., its occasion, intensity, volume, and duration). In this instance, the gap between the natural and the semiotic aspects of laughter is exposed. The laughter of the court is "stage laughter": *"The court bursts into very shrill but very well orchestrated laughter. It is not free and easy laughter"* (p. 9). Orchestrated laughter is laughter "within quotation marks," semiotized laughter, implying a meaning that derives from a *code,* rather than from nature. The point is driven home by a further elaboration: the "laughter" of the court *"is echoed by the same but even shriller laughter of the Negroes"* (p. 9). This echoed—or imitated—laughter, being the imitation of an imitation, the sign of a sign, has as its primary effect the inundation or coopting of the "real" or "natural" realm by the artificial or semiotic realm: in short, semiotization. (The fact that the phenomenon thus semiotized is one of the traditional "rights" of the audience, a source of the expression of its independence from and control over the play in progress, is relevant to the work's analysis of the audience-performer relationship, which I will discuss later.)

The semiotization principle of theatrical discourse is itself a result of a very basic mechanism of theatrical semiosis: *second-order* or *bilevel* signification. It is this mechanism which accounts for the paradox of the "offstage gesture." A theatrical gesture is a sign which stands for the conventionally established correlation between a certain body movement and a certain meaning. Thus an actor's raised and outstretched hand is a material sign-vehicle (or signifier) which the spectator will, on the basis of his knowledge of social kinesic codes, correlate with the concept "stop." The movement will become a *theatrical* gesture when the spectator, on the basis of his knowledge of the theatrical code (i.e., his theatrical "competence"), will read it as meaning not the *actor's* but the *character's* desire to cause someone or something to stop. The process (which is conceptual, not temporal) whereby a material sign-vehicle attains dramatic meaning can be diagrammed as follows:

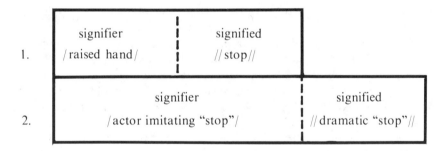

The first level in the diagram represents the physical production of a sign, as it would be produced in society. The second level maps the transformation of the social sign into a theatrical sign, with a dramatic signified. Both of these "levels" are in fact contexts, or systems, and can be variously designated (for example: denotation and connotation).

Thus all theatrical signs, including gestures, are dependent on not one but two contexts—the social and the theatrical—both of which must be shared by the spectator. (Failures to read a sign are frequently not due simply to unfamiliarity with the theatrical convention but to unfamiliarity with the *social* code upon which it is based. For example, an African audience may fail to gain the connotation "evil" or "incest" from the marriage of Gertrude and Claudius, because their kinship codes *require* that a man wed his brother's widow: such a marriage is, in itself, sufficient to characterize the man as a good man, instead of—as in Western society—signaling something unnatural and suspect, being a violation of the kinship code.)

The capacity of containment peculiar to drama, its ability to sustain various "worlds" within it, makes it a kind of paradigm for an ontological inquiry. The fact that a play creates a world has, as Keir Elam notes, been noticed and documented, but hardly explained: "Innumerable attempts have been made by critics to explore and describe individual dramatic worlds and their inhabitants (say, the world of *Macbeth* or of *Ghosts*), at least as they appear in written texts, but relatively little attention has been paid to their peculiar logical and ontological status. One of the tasks of a poetics of the drama is to explicate the general 'world-creating' principles of dramatic representation."[9]

Any attempt to "explore and describe" the dramatic "world" of *The Blacks* will immediately find itself self-confronted, as one is in looking into a mirror. For *The Blacks* is, precisely, an investigation of the dramatic world, not merely its own but all dramatic worlds; that is, it is an analysis of the nature of dramatic worlds. Only by disregarding the "performance" level of the play and focusing on the "fiction performed" level can one even begin to characterize this world. Most critical readings of the play have done precisely this, treating Virtue and Village, for instance, as straightforward dramatic characters rather than as what they are: dramatic representations of dramatic characters.[10] Taken as a totality, however, the play quite aggressively *denies* the existence of any stable dramatic world within it. It might be objected that this very denial is the play's dramatic world, a kind of nonworld or illusion of the sort Pirandello was so good at evoking. But Genet is not Pirandello; he succeeds in actually escaping the usual limits of metatheater, which is "doomed" to be theater no matter how far it carries its self-reflexivity.

In place of a dramatic world, or even (as in Pirandello) a theatrical-dramatic world, Genet succeeds in bringing into being (for the duration of the performance) a reality that is absolute, that exists both inside *and outside* the theatrical realm, and that implicates the total identities of the spectators and the actors: that is, it involves them as real people, not just as "roles" or "functions" as is customary in theatrical experience. This absolute reality that the play creates is a function of a series of codings, recodings, and decodings, the "action" of the play being an interplay of codes (or, to use Erving Goffman's term, "frames")[11] which are put into varying and complex relationships with each other.

The central rule of the dramatic frame, according to Goffman, "is that the audience has neither the right nor the obligation to participate directly in the dramatic action occurring on the stage."[12] However, there is a reason for this rule which constitutes another rule, perhaps even more "central" than the one just mentioned. This is the rule or understanding that the dramatic realm is completely separate from the world of praxis.[13] Indeed, the theatrical frame can be conceived of as an imaginary line that divides two realities—the symbolic and the practical.

Gregory Bateson, from whom the concept of frame derives, distinguishes two kinds of activity: serious and unserious.[14] "Unserious" activities are activities that are not intended to be taken literally, and that have no external and unforeseeable consequences. The ability to engage in such activities, which entails a recognition of signals *as* signals, strikes Bateson as a "very important stage in evolution."[15] Once it is realized that a sign is different from the thing it stands for, and can therefore "be trusted, distrusted, falsified, denied, amplified, corrected and so forth,"[16] once, that is, that it becomes possible to lie, a whole new arena of social behavior comes into existence. This arena might be called "make-believe" or, as Bateson calls it, "play."

Play differs from "serious" activities in that it requires that its participants be "capable of some degree of metacommunication—i.e., of exchanging signals which would carry the message 'this is play.' "[17] Bateson's formulation of the metamessage "this is play," although based on the playing of games by animals and humans, nicely captures the bilevel-signification characteristic of theatrical semiosis as well: "These actions, in which we now engage, do not denote what would be denoted by those actions which these actions denote."[18] In terms of animal play: "the playful nip denotes the bite, but it does not denote what would be denoted by the bite [namely, hostility]."[19] In terms of theater: the red liquid on an actor's shirt denotes blood, but it does not denote (to the spectator) what would be denoted by blood, namely, that the *actor* is wounded and in pain. All these it *connotes*, or denotes, *of the character* whom the actor is representing.

Bateson's formulation, when applied to theater, focuses attention on the point of contact between the two levels of theatrical signification: by being mediated through the first level (the theatrical), the second level (the dramatic) loses the practical force associated with the reality it otherwise resembles in every (visible) way. The audience—and this is why this is the "frame"— has a firm grasp of this mechanism, and will not, unless forced, confused or deliberately misled, mistake a played action for the action it denotes. Thus a stage corpse may look exactly like a real dead body, but the audience will not try to have it removed before it starts to rot, or have its killer arrested. It will know that the corpse's "existence" will end at the end of the play, when the actor rises to take his bow. (Genet's corpses always demonstrate their "inframe" existence in one way or another.)

The semiotic formula of play thus applies to onstage activity, making performance seem analogous to the make-believe games children play. In his article on theater semiotics, Umberto Eco offers precisely this analogy, describing an incident from a Borges novel in which the Arab philosopher Averroes, pondering the meaning of the words "comedy" and "tragedy" in Aristotle's *Poetics,* "is disturbed by some noise coming from downstairs. On the patio a group of boys are playing. One of them says, 'I am the Muezzin,' and climbs on the shoulders of another one, who is pretending to be a minaret. Others are representing the crowd of believers."[20] Averroes, of course, fails to recognize the connection between this behavior and Aristotle's subject, and Eco ends his essay by stressing that connection: "But the theatrical performance has begun before—when *Averroes was peeping at* the boy who was saying, 'I am the Muezzin.'"[21]

Eco is careful to introduce the element of "watching" into his definition of theater, and this is crucial. For a theatrical performance differs from a child's fantasy game in this precise respect: it is engaged in not primarily for the enjoyment it provides its *performers* but for the benefit of its *spectators.* Moreover, this "display" purpose in theater is well understood by all concerned. (Thus Eco is wrong: the muezzin incident is *not* theater, since neither from the boys' point of view nor from Averroes's is it intended for display.) Thus a play is less "play" than "show."

This being the case, the theatrical situation as a whole, the interaction not just between performers on stage but between actors and spectators, is less easily defined as "play." Of course, it could be said that a theatrical event is a game played by two teams, the performers and the spectators, its main rule being that the former pretend ignorance of the latter's presence, while the latter believe, temporarily, any fictional actions the former are "playing at." But this is unsatisfactory: for it is not the actors but the *characters* who are ignorant of the audience's presence (the actors *do,* sometimes, pretend ignorance, but not always, indeed, not usually), and the audience never believes, not even temporarily, in the fiction (if it did, the nonpraxis condition would not exist, and well-meaning spectators would be storming the stage to fight villains and protect innocents).

If it is not play, what then is the mode of spectator-performer interaction? It is not play (at least not totally) because it is largely *not* nonliteral: there is a literal *economic exchange,* there are literal *social roles* (many actors are actors by *profession*: their activity is therefore serious, not just a pleasant unserious way to spend their leisure time), and it engages literal *human experiences* like love, hate, revenge, incest, forgery, and syphilis.

Yet, perhaps because of the illusionistic nature of drama (especially of Western drama), the literal aspects of theater are usually ignored (or relegated to the sociology of theater, outside semiosis), and the play model is widely—if tacitly—accepted. Even modern metatheater ignores this area, meandering, by way of semiotic focus, into a fog of pseudophilosophical trivialities about the illusion of reality and the reality of illusion. The problem with metatheatricality is that, while attempting to "break" its frame, all it does is reframe itself even more strongly. As Susan Sontag writes of the filmmaker Godard, a dedicated metafilmist:

> In *La Chinoise,* Godard makes the point about its being a movie by, among other devices, flashing the clapper board on the screen from time to time, and by briefly cutting to Raoul Coutard, the cameraman on this as on most of Godard's films, seated behind his apparatus.
>
> But then one immediately imagines some underling holding another clapper while the scene was shot, and someone else who had to be there behind another camera to photograph Coutard. It's impossible ever to penetrate behind the final veil and experience cinema unmediated by cinema. [22]

The same impossibility has appeared to obtain in the theater, but only because the focus of metatheatrical works has been theatrical semiosis instead of theater itself. This is where Genet's *The Blacks* differs from the metatheatrical genre in which it is usually placed. For beyond theatrical semiosis, the play seeks to tackle theatrical reality itself—the literal actors and spectators, and their literal relationship.

This is an awesome task, for it involves not only a departure from traditional metatheatrical practice (of the sort associated with Pirandello) but also a challenge to a fairly widespread tendency, in our time, to apply a dramatic model (albeit an imprecise and unsophisticated one) to a variety of social, political, and psychological phenomena. [23] The power of the dramatic model is especially noticeable in the social sciences, for example in works like Goffman's *The Presentation of Self in Everyday Life,* which analyzes social "roles" and "role-playing."

This coopting of drama by the social sciences, which *literally* makes all the world a stage, may explain the surge of metatheater in modern drama. But whereas the dramatic model has proved its explanatory power in the social sciences, it seems to lead theater, paradoxically, to a sterile dead end, a hall of empty mirrors.

Genet's *The Blacks,* by its insistence on real black actors and real white spectators, puts the image back into the mirror and—after much metatheatrical derealizing and distancing—brings about a real confrontation between real people. In Goffman's terms, it employs a series of frame breaks until it shatters the frame altogether, or enlarges it to such dimensions that it becomes irrelevant.

In Bateson's terms, the play surreptitiously exchanges its "play" status for that of a form of behavior resembling play but very different from it motivationally: threat: "Threat is another phenomenon which resembles play in that actions denote, but are different from, other actions. The clenched fist of threat is different from the punch, but it refers to a possible future (but at present non-existent) punch." [24] This similarity can lead to a shift in, or confusion of, models, as when the metacommunicative message "This is play" becomes "Is this play?" (Bateson cites hazing as an example of this mode of nonliteral behavior.) *The Blacks* makes precisely this kind of modal shift.

The Blacks is structured as a series of progressively inclusive and frequently overlapping staged interactions (which we may call microplays) each of which can be thought of as existing in a different "world" from some of the others or, in semiotic terms, as messages framed in different codes. The main codes employed are the metatheatrical, the dramatic, the mimetic, the diegetic, the ritualistic, and the pantomimic—many of which, of course, overlap with each other (e.g., the mimetic and diegetic codes are regular subcodes of the dramatic code; few dramatic worlds could come into being without both these subcodes). Before the interaction of these codes can be studied, it is well to list the various realms they create and operate, with a few brief comments on each distinguishable realm.

Within the macroplay—the play entitled *The Blacks*—the following microplays (many of which seep into each other on occasion) can be identified:

1. The performance-audience interaction, across the "footlights." This "play," handled almost exclusively by the character Archibald in his role as master of ceremonies, is the most obviously metatheatrical. The mode of dramatic discourse it employs is direct address, with, as we will see, interesting variations on the traditional form and use of that device. One of the main functions of this "play" is to semiotize the audience, making it play the *role* of an audience, which means, paradoxically, making it *perform* (as audience) within the macroplay of which it is also the audience.

2. The stage actors–stage audience interaction. This "play," which appears simply to be a "staged" version of (1), is complicated by its motivational ambiguity. While seeming to be simply a "play within a play" (a device that usually entails the division of performers into "actors" and "audience"), it turns out to be, in fact, a collusion, by which the real audience is the excluded entity. This is managed by means of an unorthodox deployment of "information" and "information states" in the play, which I shall discuss later. This interaction also affords the clearest example of the delicate "communication status" that is typical of the various instances of make-believe in the play: all the "microplays" waver between the motivational modes (or "frames") of play, deceit, and threat.

3. Various interactions among members of the "performing group" (i.e., those who play "actors" in (2)). These interactions range from the metatheatrical (discussions on how to perform play (5)) to the intensely dramatic (the love affair between Village and Virtue).

4. *Various interactions among the members of the stage "audience,"* usually in a blatantly theatrical mode. The tension in these interactions is located in the actors themselves; they are Negroes masked as whites, capturing the theme of racial conflict in the sign-vehicle itself: the actual actor.

5. *The murder of the white woman.* This "play," a play-within-plays (1) and (2) and a play-alongside-plays (3) and (4), employs a variety of codes: ritual, mimesis, pantomime, and diegesis. It involves unequal transformations of performers into characters (Village plays himself, Diouf plays the white woman, Village plays the white woman's voice).

This play is presented with extremely ambiguous motivations: at one extreme, it is a powerful and efficacious ritual, the source of black self-actualization; at another, it is an empty charade, a hoax, a mere distraction.

6. *The offstage play.* This is, in reference to play (1), a play-*outside*-the-play. It consists of the trial and execution of a Negro (whose ontological status is extremely problematic) by comrades of the performers and is revealed gradually to be the raison d'être of play (1), but linked to it only by fraud and deceit, not dramatic causality. This nonplay, to the "performance" of which the audience is tauntingly denied access, attains the highest level of dramatic reality. Although this play is, of course, a fiction, its subtle relationship to the performance—in terms both of theme and structure—makes it, finally, "real"—more real than the macroplay itself. Indeed, the macroplay becomes, by the end, a device for the assertion of this "real," outside reality, one that the audience experiences in a far more personal (and real) way than is normal. Another way of putting this: play (6) becomes the signified of the macrosignifier known as *The Blacks,* and has a real *referent* in cultural reality (namely, racism).

The preceding statements, I am aware, will hardly be intelligible before I have gone through an analysis of the whole play. Before doing that, however, I will simply offer one observation that will suggest the peculiar role of racial matters in the play. It is this: racism is not merely a *theme* of *The Blacks,* it is the play's *reality.* Genet, it is well known, is dedicated to exposing appearances on stage. With regard to *The Maids,* for instance, he intimated that an ideal production of the play would be one in which *male* actors would play the roles of Solange and Claire (the two female characters who spend the whole play role-playing). Sartre provides the following explanation for Genet's apparently excessive demand for "total" role-playing:

One might be tempted to explain this demand by Genet's taste for young boys. Nevertheless, this is not the essential reason. The truth of the matter is that Genet wishes from the very start to *strike at the root of the apparent*. No doubt an actress can play Solange, but what might be called the "derealizing" would not be radical, since there would be no need to play at being a woman.... It is not Solange who is to be a theatrical illusion, but rather *the woman Solange*.[25]

Given this history, is it not surprising that Genet did not call for the black characters in *The Blacks* to be played by white actors (in blackface)? In the case of the stage "audience," who wear white masks, this would have made for a delightful double derealization: whites in blackface wearing white masks. (It would also have engaged all the negative connotations that the blackface device now has.) Yet he did not: in fact, he goes out of his way to stress that the play should be performed by real blacks, for a white audience. The choice might be explained as a matter of political commitment, or, to paraphrase Sartre, by Genet's taste for the colonized and the oppressed. The real reason, however, is a theatrical one, although almost the opposite of the motive for having the Maids played by male actors. In *The Blacks* it is "re-realization" that Genet is after, not "derealization." The curious thing about the play is that, in spite of its metatheatrical frame (play (1)), the confrontation it entails is both theatrical/dramatic *and real*: actual blacks and whites confront each other, and their actuality is the "ground" against which the drama unfolds.

The reality of the black actors is emphasized throughout the play. One of Archibald's first tasks as master of ceremonies is to "introduce" his "actors," who are asked to take a bow as their names are called. One of them, Snow, proves uncooperative, and provides Archibald (and Genet) with the opportunity to expose the gap between performance and reality:

ARCHIBALD: Mrs. Augusta Snow (*she remains upright*)...well...Madam (*roaring angrily*) bow! (*she remains upright*)...I'm asking you, madam, to bow! (*extremely gentle, almost grieved*) I'm asking you, Madam to bow—it's a *performance* (*she bows*).
(p. 10; my emphasis)

A little later, Archibald makes the following revelation about his troupe: "When we leave this stage, we are involved in your life, I am a cook, this lady is a sewing maid, this gentleman is a medical student, this gentleman is a curate at St. Anne's...." (p. 14). This acknowledgement of (alleged) offstage identity is one of several instances in the play where the related concepts of "person" and "role" are discussed. It matters little that the "real personhood" asserted in this speech is fictional ("Liars that we are, the names I have mentioned are false" (p. 14)); the point that a bifurcation exists between a person and his role has been made and woven into the fabric of the play. It will remain productive throughout the performance, and behind every role played before us will lurk an unidentified real person. Thus when Village begins his oration on the murder he has committed, his theatrical discourse will appear to be constantly shadowed and threatened by a real experience, made all the more real by virtue of its careful exclusion from the fiction:

ARCHIBALD: Be careful, Village, don't start referring to your real life.

(p. 35)

ARCHIBALD: Don't allude to your life.

(p. 38)

BOBO: ... There's no need for us to know about your personal sufferings and dislikes. That's *your* business ... in your room.

(p. 38)

The most powerful "reality" is, of course, the one lived by these black actors: as blacks in a white society, actually engaged in a real race war and a real revolution that is occurring in secret, unknown to the white enemy, who is being carefully distracted from it by role-playing (of both the theatrical and the social variety).

This "offstage reality," which I have called play (6), is, of course, fictional. But everything in the play is directed towards asserting that this fiction is an imitation of reality, and that the reality it imitates is all around; it is both the sociocultural context and the true subject of the macroplay under way. It is constantly flooding into the macroplay, and seems to be continuous with, instead of disjunct from, the dramatic fiction. This violation of the traditional separation of fiction and reality is summed up nicely in a comment of Archibald's, in which the metatheatrical, the dramatic, and the theatrical mingle strangely in a single discursive unit: "Tonight our sole concern will be to entertain you. So we have killed this white woman. There she lies." (*He points to the catafalque*) (p. 14).

The developing reality of the black performers is, to a large degree, a function of a peculiar reality the play bestows on the audience. Just as Genet insists on real black actors, he insists on real white spectators:

This play, written, I repeat, by a white man, is intended for a white audience, but if, which is unlikely, it is ever performed before a black audience, then a white person, male or female, should be invited every evening. The organizer of the show should welcome him formally, dress him in ceremonial costume and lead him to his seat, preferably in the front row of the orchestra. The actors will play for him. A spotlight should be focused upon this symbolic white throughout the performance.

But what if no white person accepted? Then let white masks be distributed to the black spectators as they enter the theater. And if the blacks refuse the masks, then let a dummy be used.

(p. 4)

It is my contention that a real white audience—not masked blacks, not a "symbolic white," not a "dummy"—is essential to the logic of the play. Without such an audience, a quite different play would result. (Perhaps another way of looking at this is that there are several T-Texts in this one script: one with a white audience, one with a mixed audience, one with a "symbolic white" spectator, one with masked black spectators, one with a white dummy spectator. Far from being equal and interchangeable, these audiences make for totally different theatrical experiences. In this essay I will discuss the "ideal case" only: the T-Text that contains a real white audience.)

The impact of the audience on the performance is a curious, perhaps unique feature of *The Blacks*. In insisting on a certain kind of audience, Genet goes far beyond the traditional "rights" of the playwright, whose control of a performance is supposed to be restricted to the onstage activity. By flaunting this conventional restriction, Genet raises some interesting semiotic questions, and achieves some powerful effects.

First of all, there is the question of the relationship between the sender and the receiver of the theatrical message. If a play is a message, then it follows that it is *intended* for a certain interpreter or reader. But for this to be the case, i.e., for such an intention to exist, the sender must have some knowledge of the receiver, of his capacity to receive. He must first mentally "constitute" the receiver before sending him the message. Now theatrical messages, like everyday verbal ones, are usually sent to a receiver who is unconsciously preconstituted by the sender. Thus the playwright writes for an "audience," by which is really meant: an anonymous group of people who possess (more or less) the same social and theatrical codes as the playwright. These shared codes are usually unconscious, internalized through social experience. Thus the playwright can set his play in the distant past without risking that it will appear odd, old-fashioned, out-of-date (= dramatic code). Or he can call for a stage whisper without risking that the audience will think that every character on stage had heard the whisper (= theatrical code).

The question of "intended audience" becomes clearer in the case of special theatrical types, such as children's theater. Here the playwright must be more conscious of the codes he employs, since his audience cannot be expected to have the same social and theatrical competence as himself. Other "special audiences"—such as a prison audience, a college audience, or an all-gay audience—also enjoin a special attention to the codes employed, and allow for a more particular communication than usual.

The Blacks, insofar as it specifies its intended audience, would seem to be a case of "special audience." Yet the quality called for in this audience is far from special: most members of Western audiences *are* white. Why, then, does Genet make such a point of this very usual characteristic? The answer lies in the traditional "role" of the audience, a role which calls for the transformation of a person into (1) an anonymous member of a group and (2) an onlooker.

Firstly, by insisting on the *whiteness* of the audience, the play obliterates the distinction between spectator-as-person and spectator-as-role. The spectator role (or rather that part of the spectator role that Goffman calls "theater-goer")[26] involves a certain degree of *depersonalization* (the individual ceases to be an individual and becomes part of a mass entity) and of *anonymity.* The play is addressed not to the specific people present but to anyone who might happen to occupy the seats. As such, the specific people can, for the duration, abandon their specific identities, along with all the roles and attributes that constitute these identities. They can attend merely as spectators, and need not fear that their "personalities" will be engaged in any direct or intentional way. (These personalities may, however, be engaged indirectly and unintentionally: for example, a spectator who has recently lost her father may find Ophelia's mad scene unbearable to watch as a mere spectator. Interestingly, *Hamlet* contains one of the few examples of *intentional* engagement of a spectator's specific personality:

> I have heard
> That guilty creatures sitting at a play
> Have by the very cunning of the scene
> Been struck so to the soul that presently
> They have proclaimed their malefactions....
>   I'll have these players
> Play something like the murder of my father
> Before mine uncle. I'll observe his looks.
> I'll tent him to the quick. If 'a do blench
> I know my course.
>
> (act 2, sc. 2, lines 575–84))

The anonymity condition of spectatorship appears to be unbreachable. Direct address does not violate it, not even, according to some, direct address which deals not with some fictional reality (as direct address usually does) but with the spectators themselves: "The dramatic world can be extended to include the 'author', the 'audience' and even the 'theater'; but these remain 'possible' surrogates, not the 'actual' referents as such (even the public insulted by Handke's characters is a virtual rather than real entity, however genuinely taken aback the audience may be)."[27] This is probably true so long as the terms remain theatrical (Handke insults the audience *as audience*) but not when they are not. In *The Blacks,* the audience is constantly reminded of an aspect of its "personhood" that it considers irrelevant to its role as spectator, an attribute of its personal identity which it usually thinks it has left behind at home: its whiteness. The forcible inclusion of this personality element into the performance matrix is extremely disturbing. It shakes the audience's sense of its control over the theatrical "frame," and makes it impossible to participate in the event merely as theatergoers. (This is the first method by which the message "This is play" is slowly transformed into its opposite: "This is not play. We are blacks. You are whites. The conflict we are staging actually exists between yourselves and us.")

Nor is the role of "theatergoer" the only spectator role being challenged. The other aspect of the spectator role—"the onlooker"[28]—is also questioned and discredited. At several points in the play Archibald cautions his "actors" to be careful, guarded, for "we're being watched" (p. 29). The onlooker role of the audience is thus *foregrounded*, but it is also *parodied* (by the stage "audience") and *twisted*. The fact of "being watched," which is traditionally a necessary condition of dramatic representation, is regarded here as a *threat*: the "show" or "display" quality of drama is transformed into its opposite: concealment. The audience's primary right to perceive everything within its evidential boundaries is, if not denied, surely abridged. For what the audience sees and hears is, besides avowedly being a "performance," also implicitly a *fraud*, deliberately perpetrated to mask or conceal a "true" state of affairs unfolding elsewhere. This true state is never dramatized, although we get diegetic glimpses of it through the character Newport News:

> ARCHIBALD: (*going up to Newport News*): Well? Has anything happened yet?
> NEWPORT NEWS: He's arrived. We've brought him along, handcuffed.
> SNOW: What are you going to do?
> NEWPORT NEWS: (*bending down and picking up a revolver from the shoeshine box*): First of all, question him.
> ARCHIBALD: (*interrupting*): Say only what you have to. We're being watched. (*They all look up at the Court.*)
>
> (pp. 28–29; my emphasis)

The relationship between what the audience witnesses and what it is vaguely aware of occurring "offstage" (i.e., between microplays (1–5) and microplay (6)) appears to be nondramatic, a relationship of parallelism instead of cause:

> ARCHIBALD (*to Newport News*): ... Go tell them. Let them know we've started. *They're to do their job just as we'll do ours.*
>
> (p. 16; my emphasis)

The idea that the performance is a "job" (in some way similar to a job being done somewhere else by cohorts of the "actors") is underlined by all the metatheatrical apparatus and commentary surrounding the enactment of the ritual (play 5). Every aspect of performance is discussed: the event is a "performance" ("This evening we will perform for you" (p. 12)); the people are *actors,* their skin is *makeup* ("In order to serve you, [we] shall use our beautiful shiny black makeup. It is Mr. Deodatus Village who gathers the smoke-black and Mrs. Felicity Trollop Pardon who thins it out in our saliva" (p. 10)); the flowers are *props* ("They're there for the performances. Which doesn't require that you burst into bloom. Put back the iris" (p. 15)) and speech is *script* ("Go right ahead, since our speeches are set down in the script" (p. 29)). Moreover, there is constant verbalization of what Bateson calls "regulators"—the unspoken conventions that allow a message to proceed. In *The Blacks,* characters frequently "pass" speeches/action to each other, along with speaking directions:

> ARCHIBALD: You take it, Virtue. And roll them out, high and clear.
>
> SNOW (*to Bobo*): Take it.
> BOBO: Let's both take it!...
> ARCHIBALD: All right. Take it, Village.

(pp. 56–58)

Besides "regulators," "directives" are also articulated:

> THE VALET: As for that last sentence, it oughtn't to be rolled off as if it were a proclamation.
> (p. 13)
>
> VILLAGE: That the right tone?
> (p. 59)

Other "out-of-frame" elements of performance are also drawn into the frame; for instance, *costume* is referred to in a way that reveals both its dramatic necessity and its semiotic nature:

> VILLAGE: But he's not wearing a skirt!... I'll stop my speech if you don't put a skirt on him.
> ARCHIBALD: Snow, your shawl....
> (p. 59)

Casting, about which I will have more to say later, is another preperformance phenomenon that this performance includes:

> VILLAGE: You realize I'm supposed to re-enact it. I need a straight man.... Who'll help me? Who? After all, it doesn't much matter who.
> (p. 53)

Although the reason given for this lack of relevance of person to role is that "the whites can hardly distinguish one Negro from another" (p. 53), another— semiotic—reason also exists: in the theater, signs are "free"; anything or anyone can signify anything or anyone.

All this metatheatrical commentary has a strange effect on the audience's experience. It tends to move the performance away from a "pure" state and closer to the state of what Goffman calls "work performances": "those that occur, for example, at construction sites *or rehearsals,* where viewers openly watch persons at work who openly show no regard or concern for the dramatic elements of their labor" (my emphasis).[29] *The Blacks* is, of course, a "staged" work performance, but it nevertheless disturbs the status of the audience. It places the audience in the position of people watching the *preparations* for a performance at which they are to be the audience: the result is a "frame" confusion, which makes it hard to select those elements which are relevant to them as "onlookers" and disregard (dramatically) those which are not.

The "onlooker" status of the audience is further deconstructed by the presence of the stage "audience," which constantly parodies audience response, forcing the drama down into the auditorium. An example of this is the "laughter" I have already mentioned, and its stage use reveals its semiotic/syntactical nature:

> The difference between theater-goer and onlooker is nicely illustrated in regard to laughter, demonstrating again the need to be very clear about the syntax of response. Laughter by members of the audience in sympathetic response to an effective bit of buffoonery is clearly distinguished on both sides of the stage line from audience laughter that can greet an actor who flubs, trips or breaks up in some unscripted way. In the first case the individual laughs as onlooker, in the second as theater-goer.[30]

In the play, the stage "audience" laughs in response to Archibald's formal opening, "Ladies and Gentlemen," a situation that calls for neither kind of laughter, since it is neither intentionally nor unintentionally funny. The laughter becomes, consequently, a sign of semiotic failure, of inappropriateness. Other signs for the same phenomenon are the non sequiturs on stock prices that the "audience" often breaks into: "Eastern Ubangi 1,580. Saint Johnny-get-your-gun 1,050. Macupia 2,002. M'Zaita 20, 008" (p. 19). These inappropriate "responses" are *syntactically* wrong (or "ungrammatical") but, for that very reason, they are semantically significant. They signify the "audience's" (and, by reflection, the audience's) *fear* of what they are witnessing (they occur typically at moments of high tension and threat) as well as their ideological background in economic imperialism. The cultural aspect of this ideology is "exoticism,"[31] also dramatized in various "audience" comments on the "performers": "They're exquisitely spontaneous. They have a strange beauty. Their flesh is weightier. . . ." (p. 19). Both the economic and the cultural aspects of this ideology are projected onto the real audience (of which the masked court is a stage version), who is thus integrated into the drama. This integration of the real and the dramatic is made possible by the play's metatheatricality, its status as a performed performance, because economic and cultural exploitation of blacks is a fact not only of life but of this play as well: the audience has "bought" a right to watch blacks be blacks. The stage audience's behavior is consequently a replica of its real counterpart, which becomes therefore—forcibly—part of the drama. Again: the staged confrontation is a sign for a real one, and its referent is present in the auditorium.

Being a series of disjunct "plays" rather than a single, coherent play, *The Blacks* begins again and again. It begins when the curtain is drawn back, when Archibald says "Ladies and Gentlemen," when Village starts to discuss his crime, when Village and Diouf begin to enact the crime, when the court arrives in "Africa," when the Queen and Felicity begin their rhetorical battle, when the defeated Court begins its series of suicides, and even when, in the final moments, the backdrop rises to reveal the cast standing around another catafalque. The final beginning is, of course, a replica of the first one: the play comes full circle. Being without the traditional division into acts and scenes, *The Blacks* is articulated by these many beginnings; the command "Begin" echoes throughout it.

The script of *The Blacks* begins with a curious and emphatic stage direction: "The curtain is drawn. Not raised—drawn" (p. 7). It is a measure of Genet's total interest in theater and theatrical convention that even as trivial a convention as this is semiotized, to demonstrate that it is perhaps not so trivial after all.

Generally, no semiotic difference is felt to exist between a drawn curtain and a raised one. The two are equivalent material signifiers for the temporal aspect of the theatrical "frame." Like certain other signals that frequently accompany it, such as the dimming of the house lights, the sounding of clappers or dull hammers, the curtain's removal marks the liminal moment between play and not-play, fiction and reality, and (from the point of view of audience behavior) theatergoing and play-watching.

In *The Blacks* this conventional use of the curtain is, we might say, *over*used. The first curtain, the one that is to be *drawn,* is put into opposition with another "curtain"—the backdrop, which, near the end, is *raised.* Thus the play ends with the raising of a new curtain—a new "beginning." The audience must leave when this "play" begins.

Besides this structural significance, the curtains of the play also acquire a *semantic* significance. If the backdrop, an element of the décor system, can become a curtain, so too can other elements, from other systems. Examples of these abound, all acquiring meaning from the curtain paradigm with its "concealed-revealed" axis:

Concealment / Revelation: Other "Curtains"

1. The Backdrop: a "curtain" borrowed from the system "décor"—usually a spatial aspect of the play's frame, marking the visual-evidence boundary, this one is (i) turned into a temporal marker and (ii) redefined spatially as *within* the visual-evidence boundary, which is now marked by another backdrop. This second backdrop will naturally, by transitivity, acquire the same ambiguity as the first. The effect of this curtain is to give the stage endless (implied) depth—backstages of backstages (stretching out of the theater?).

2. *The Catafalque:* a "curtain" borrowed from the "furnishings" system. The catafalque does not in fact "exist," a fact that does not prevent it from having a full theatrical and dramatic existence during a large part of the play. This is a good demonstration of the nature of theatrical signs, which, even when concrete (say, a chair), are primarily signs ("A chair on the stage is a theater chair"—Peter Handke).[32] This catafalque happens to be made of chairs, which have "existed" before they are seen, as "missing" props.[33] In fact, the Court's first reaction to the discredited catafalque is not to its emptiness but to its *contents*; "My chairs!" exclaims the Queen. "They were there all the time," says the Valet (p. 96). This is literally as well as theatrically true, since the chairs have been in the play, by virtue of their (discussed) absence, "all the time."

The case of the absent-present chairs relates to an important aspect of theatrical semiotics—what Keir Elam calls the "world-creating" capacity of dramatic discourse. "In the absence of narratorial guides, providing external description and 'world-creating' propositions, the dramatic world has to be specified *from within* by means of references made to it by the very individuals who constitute it."[34] This self-actualizing method is clearly seen in *The Blacks,* which is *about* the creation (and subsequent discrediting) of a dramatic world. Like the chairs which are brought into dramatic existence by means of a discussion of their absence, the corpse, which is *really* absent, is "created" by means of an extended discussion of its nature as theatrical "prop":

> VILLAGE: You forget that I'm already knocked out from the crime I had to finish off before you arrived, since you need a fresh corpse for every performance....
> DIOUF: ...Actually, we *could* use the same corpse a number of times. Its presence is the thing.
> ARCHIBALD: What about the odor, Mr. Vicar General?
>
> (pp. 19–20)

Whether this corpse is a "fresh" one or a stale one, that it is *there* is stressed—"its presence is the thing." This presence, however, is a function of repeated indexical (pointing) and deictic ("it," "that," "her") reference. When the catafalque is exposed as an empty structure, the gap between theatrical reality and dramatic reality gapes wide. It is a gap that is usually revealed only out-of-frame, before or after the play, when the stage is being set or struck. Here, the drama incorporates this out-of-frame reality, and the disastrous effect is articulated by the stage "audience":

THE JUDGE: ... There was no one in the packing case ... tell us why.

ARCHIBALD (*sadly*): Alas, your Honor, there was no packing case either.

THE GOVERNOR: No packing case? No packing case either? They kill us without killing us and shut us up in no packing case either!

THE MISSIONARY: After that dodge, they won't be able to say they don't fake. *They've been stringing us along.*

(p. 98; my emphasis)

The play's mode is not play but deceit. Just like the murdered white woman whose "death wasn't meant to signify merely that she lost her life" (p. 17), the empty catafalque is not meant to signify merely that no death has occurred: only that there is not—there cannot be—a real corpse on stage. But "elsewhere," perhaps in the second catafalque, perhaps *in one behind that,* perhaps there is a real corpse, the ultimate "referent" of all these signs and signs of signs. On stage one must content oneself with "killing a white woman who's already dead" (p. 31), but "elsewhere," "it's a matter of living blood, hot, supple, reeking blood, *of blood that bleeds...*" (p. 82; my emphasis). Somewhere, beyond all the performances, behind all the backstages, there is "a *serious* affair ... no longer a matter of staging a performance" (p. 81; my emphasis). This is the real world, to which all the dramatic worlds of the play ultimately refer.

3. The Masks. In the taxonomy of theatrical signs, the mask occupies a curious position: it is the point at which two distinct theatrical sign systems—makeup and facial expression—overlap. Moreover, the mask can be—and for long has been—thought of as the theatrical sign *par excellence,* for it is the perfect example of the simultaneously concealing and revealing nature of theater. It hides one reality (the actor's face) and displays another (the character's face), the latter being "grafted" onto the former by means of a convention everyone understands and accepts. The mask is thus the *actor's* "curtain," and the *character's* "stage": a temporary, fictional reality put on display for the audience.

The masks worn by the Court in *The Blacks* are worn not so much as "fictional faces" but *as masks,* underlining their dual and contradictory (revealing-concealing) nature: *"Each actor playing a member of the court is a masked Negro whose mask represents the face of a white person. The mask is worn in such a way that the audience sees a wide black band all around it, and even the actor's kinky hair"* (p. 8). The point being made here—visually and concretely—is that, in the dramatic reality of the play, these actors are *actors*; only in the play-within-the-play are they members of a court. As actors, their "masks" are their faces, which can be seen around the real masks. These real masks are, consequently, masks of masks, signs of signs. The point is that, in the theater, everything is a sign; even human faces are semiotized (the familiar features of a Laurence Olivier become the sign for the face of Hamlet).

In *The Blacks*, theatrical semiotization comes full circle, and we get signs that are signs of themselves: Negro actors who play "Negro actors," masks that are "masks." When, after the offstage execution has been completed (it is managed theatrically: the dramatic signified //firing squad volley// conveyed by firecrackers which are heard and seen exploding in the wings, their sparks visible to the audience), *"the members of the Court solemnly remove their masks. The audience sees the five black faces"* (p. 111). It is as if a curtain has been lifted, but, unlike the stage curtain, this one reveals not fiction, but "reality." This lifting of the masks is equivalent to the raising of the backdrop: in both cases a new reality is exposed, and in both cases this new reality is ambiguous: one is a space containing a catafalque and / or a stage with another fake and empty structure; the other is a group of black people and / or a cast of Negro actors. The two terms of the second reality are identical, for the roles these people are playing are their real-life "roles": signifiers and signifieds have collapsed together. The implication is that this identity also obtains in the first case. Thus the whole play can be regarded as a mask for the second "play," which, like the actor-characters, has a real-life reference. The process of semiotization seems to lead, parodoxically, to desemiotization, to a *real* reality.

If the characterological function of masks and the characterological function of faces were not sufficiently revealed in the case of the Court, it is amply illustrated in the case of the actor who plays Diouf (in this role his own face is his mask) and then plays a white woman (wearing a real mask over his face-"mask"). The drama involving Diouf also provides a wonderful demonstration of the semiotics of acting, and contributes significantly to the play's process of desemiotization.

Goffman notes that "... whenever an individual participates in an episode of activity, a distinction will be drawn between what is called the person, individual or player, namely he who participates, and the particular role, capacity or function he realizes during that participation. And a connection between these two elements will be understood. In short, there will be a *person-role formula*."[35] The overall person-role formula in *The Blacks* is 1 to 1: the roles of "black actors" are played by persons who are black actors. Within the play, however, other versions of the formula obtain. For example, Diouf, who plays a black man in the macroplay, later takes the role of a white woman in microplay (5). His assumption of this role raises the question of the relationship between a person and a role: i.e., of the *rationale* of the person-role formula.

The question relates first to the phenomenon of "casting." "Given a role to be performed, what limitations are established concerning who can qualify for playing it?"[36] In the theater there are, theoretically, no limitations: since the theatrical realm is explicitly recognized as a *representation,* the "stuff" of the representing elements is irrelevant: anyone and / or anything can play anyone and/or anything. Thus a man can play a woman, a woman can play a horse, a piece of wood can play a king, a cardboard cutout can play a frying pan. The signifier-signified relationship (Sr R Sd) is (again, I stress: theoretically) absolutely free, unconstrained.

In practice, however, Sr R Sd *is* limited, governed by convention. Indeed, the code of any given type of theater is largely a matter of how it defines Sr R Sd. In realistic theater, for example, Sr R Sd is governed by iconicity, a breach of which is immediately perceived as significant. If, in a realistic play, a male plays a female, the audience will take this to mean that the male character is masquerading as a female *within the dramatic fiction.* Or the breach will produce comedy (as when Francis Flute plays Thisbe in the play-within-the-play in *A Midsummer Night's Dream*). Or some sort of metatheatrical point will seem to be being made (as in Genet's idea for *The Maids*, discussed above).

The person-role formula is, therefore, a function of convention. It is also an interesting indicator of a culture's notion of what is essential to a person (or part of the "base formula" of the person's presentation)[37] and must therefore exist in any role-version of that person. One of the most striking examples of this sense of "essence" is the attitude to race or color. It is only *very* recently that (some) audiences are beginning to accept black actors in traditionally white roles: black Hamlets (I do not mean black *Hamlets*, where all the roles are played by black actors) are only now being seen; before now the only major Shakespearean role open to a black actor was the role of Othello. What this means is that, in Western culture, color has been seen as an essential part of one's personhood, not a "role."

In the case of Diouf, we might ask why Diouf needs a *mask* to play a white; cannot his face, which after all is a "mask" for whatever character he plays, serve just as well? After all, we do not require that an actor undergo plastic surgery so as to look like a character different from himself. This is the same as asking why a white actor cannot play Othello without blackening his face: in Shakespeare's play, as in *The Blacks,* the blackness is the point, and it needs to be "actual," not virtual. It would seem that color, like, perhaps, old age, is beyond the audience's capacity for imaginative projection: it must be signified concretely and iconically.

The Western cultural bias that says that color is an essential part of a person is not merely a central theme of Genet's play, but the reality on which the play rests—the code within which it can be read as a message. Only because, to every member of Genet's white audience, color is the privileged sign in his hierarchy of person signs, only because, to them, a black man is not a man but a black man, is the play able to move beyond "play" into a realm of real, "serious" confrontation. An actual racial conflict lurks behind the "staged" one.

This real confrontation is, however, far from being regarded as a "natural" or "motivated" one: the manner in which it is brought to our notice—through a series of plays—stresses the conventional or semiotic nature even of the real (i.e., social, or real-world) racial conflict. Throughout the play, the Blacks repeatedly complain that they have to play the *roles* of blacks, not merely of black *actors* as they do in the play, but of black *people,* in their "real," offstage existence. This obligatory role-playing is forced upon them by the whites' perception of them as *primarily* black, a perception that, while based on a superficial or apparent element (the color of their skins), goes on to define them in depth:

> THE VALET: They're exquisitely spontaneous. They have a strange beauty. Their flesh is weightier.
>
> (p. 19)

The fact that here these attitudes are articulated by blacks (disguised as whites) suggests that the white concept of blacks has infected the Blacks themselves: they are subscribing to a semiotic system which is dedicated to denying their personhood and to reducing them to mere signs: "My color!" exclaims Snow, "Why, you're my very self" (p. 17). The self is overrun by the role; the sign has transformed its referent. The only path available to the Blacks by which to recover a sense of plenitude of their existence is that of acceptance, an escape not *out of* but *into* their roles:

> ARCHIBALD: Let Negroes negrify themselves. Let them persist to the point of madness in what they're condemned to be, in their ebony, in their odor, in their yellow eyes, in their cannibal tastes.
>
> (p. 52)

In a prefatory note to *The Blacks* Genet asks: "But what is a black? First of all, what is his color?" (p. 4). The play answers the question by implying that the black's color is *white,* for blackness is a concept derived from a uniquely white system which rests on the binary opposition between black and white. In playing blacks "to the point of madness" the blacks are participating in that white system, allowing it to "color" their view of everything, even of themselves.

The assumption of the role of Blacks is mapped in the play as a series of sign-appropriations. The Negroes "negrify themselves" by playing the roles associated with them: the roles of hunters, murderers, animals, even the role of a place, the African jungle: *"Very softly at first, then more and more loudly, the Negroes, almost invisible under the balcony, utter sounds of the virgin forest: croaking of the toad, hoot of the owl, a hissing, very gentle roars, breaking of wood, moaning of the wind"* (p. 92).

The rituals being enacted are seen as a means of recapturing a lost plenitude of existence, a *solid* presemiotized, preblackened/whitened self (that is now, of course, a mere memory, an image: another sign):

> VILLAGE: With my long dark strides I roamed the earth. Against that moving mass of darkness the angry but respectful sun flashed its beams. *They did not traverse my dusky bulk.* I was naked . . . The surfaces of my body were curved *mirrors on which all things were reflected*: fish, buffaloes, the laughter of tigers, reeds. . . .
>
> I was not singing. I was not dancing. Standing insolently—in short, royally—with hand on hip, I was pissing . . . I crawled through my cotton plants. The dogs sniffed me out. I bit my chains and wrists. *Slavery taught me singing and dancing.* . . . I *died* in the hold of the slave ship.
>
> (pp. 45–46; my emphasis)

Village's speech provides the "exposition," as it were, for the drama we are watching (perhaps "witnessing" is a better word, for the Blacks make it clear that their "performance"—the white woman's murder—is closer to a trial or a ritual than to a dramatic entertainment):

> ARCHIBALD: Bear one thing in mind: we must deserve their reprobation and get them to deliver the judgement that will condemn us.
>
> (p. 30)

The ritual reenactment method of self-recovery chosen by the Blacks represents a dramatic philosophy which is, in turn, rooted in a very fundamental world view. The drama they propose is a kind of Artaudian theater of cruelty, wherein everything on stage is rigorously itself, nonreferential, nonmimetic. The world view it reflects is an existentialism, whereby the role *is* the self, acting is being, and signfier and signified are identical.

In both these positions the Blacks are opposed by Diouf, an essentialist who yearns for a classical mode of drama, where beauty is born out of the artistic representation of suffering and struggle:

> DIOUF: . . . I should indeed like the performance to re-establish in our souls a balance that our plight perpetuates, *but I should like it to unfold so harmoniously that they see only the beauty of it,* and I would like them to recognize us in that beauty which disposes them to love.
>
> (p. 31; my emphasis)

Diouf is a black Aristotle, an optimistic, humanistic innocent who naively believes that the oppositional system which oppresses him and his race can be transcended by an appeal to "higher" values, by impossible compromises:

THE MISSIONARY: Tell me, my dear Vicar, what about the Host? Yes, the Host? Will you invent a black Host? And what will it be made of? Gingerbread, you say? That's brown.
DIOUF: But Monsignor, we have a thousand ingredients. We'll dye it. *A gray Host....*
THE GOVERNOR (*breaking in*): Grant the gray Host and you're sunk. You'll see—he'll demand further concessions, more oddities.
DIOUF (*plaintively*): *White on one side, black on the other?*

(p. 32; my emphasis)

It is these naively liberal tendencies that provide the "rationale" for the casting of Diouf as a *white* woman, as they do for the curiously fragmented way in which he plays that role. For, as the Mask, Diouf's playacting is restricted to pantomime: the Mask is a silent, voiceless being whose words belong to Village. As the murdered woman, Diouf is *less* than himself; as the murderer, Village is *more* than himself: he is both himself and his victim.

This fragmentation of the self, as realized in the character of the white woman, dramatizes an aspect of the person-role relationship that is crucial to acting. Erving Goffman has noted that

> when an individual is obliged to treat himself, and accept being treated, purely as a physical object, ... as when he submits to the handling of a physician, barber or cosmetician, a little joke is allowed him (one that expresses frame tension), and, more important, *complete* assimilation to object status may be something that those who are handling him will themselves deplore. In brief, individuals who are expected to make themselves available as objects are not expected to do so with abandon and ease.[38]

Diouf's role, in which he is "handled" by the actors who dress him, is an extreme case of a condition inherent in all instances of acting. The actor allows his body to be used as an object, that is, as the body of another being, the character. This total abdication of self to role (which Brechtian acting seeks to restrict by requiring the actor to keep signfication of self active alongside signification of role, thus instituting a perceptible rupture between the two parts of the character sign) is used to construct the philosophical and political theme of *The Blacks*. Diouf is not the only "actor" who becomes fragmented in the process of role-playing. The stage "audience" bears the mark of its divided existence through the play (the masks), and the "Queen" suffers a loss of signifying self similar to Diouf's. Her words are taken over by Virtue: "I am the lily-white Queen of the West..." (p. 44) until she awakens, and recites *"along with Virtue"*: "I am white, it's milk that denotes me..." (p. 45). Then, *"suddenly wide awake,"* she reappropriates her role: "That'll do! Silence them, they've stolen my voice!" (p. 46).

The constant shifting of signifieds (roles) from signifier to signifier (actors), this fluid version of identity, is a comment on the semiotic (conventional) nature of both "character" and "race": roles are constructed out of a dramatic system; blacks and whites are constructed out of a cultural system. As such, both levels of "being" are contingent on convention, as "relative" as the theater itself:

> ARCHIBALD: Since we're on stage, where everything is relative, all I need to do is walk backwards in order to create the theatrical illusion of your moving away from me.
>
> (p. 41)

In *The Blacks*, movement is stasis, sound is silence ("Village points a revolver and shoots, but there is no sound of a shot. The Governor falls" (p. 118), presence is absence (the chairs/catafalque), death is life ("Mr. Diouf, you're living a curious death" (p. 88), play is deceit, and show is concealment ("Before long, you'll see what is *hidden* behind our *display*" (p. 106; my emphasis).

The "not-play" identity of the play emerges, paradoxically, by insistence on its theatrical, "play" nature. I have already mentioned the inclusions of many "out-of-frame" elements, like directives and regulators, in the script. The play is, as it were, "shadowed" by a play in the process of being written, giving it a curiously nondramatic, distressingly "unreal," or ad hoc quality:

> THE QUEEN (*turning to the Court*): Good God, good God, what's one to say to her...
> (*The Governor, Judge, Missionary, and Valet rush up to her and whisper encouragement.*)
> THE MISSIONARY: Speak of our concern for them... of our schools....
> THE GOVERNOR: Bring up the white man's burden, quote some lines from Kipling....
>
> (p. 104)

and a little further on:

> THE QUEEN: Well? What else...
> THE GOVERNOR: Say that we have guns to silence them...
> THE MISSIONARY: That's idiotic. No, be friendly... Mention Dr. Livingstone...
>
> (p. 105)

A distinction is thus made—and made perceptible—between two levels of dramatic action: there is (1) the play we are watching and (2) the "play" the actors are performing, or constructing before our eyes. The second level appears, initially, to be contained within the first, but is gradually shown to be part of something *outside* the play we are watching, that is, we realize it is related (as smokescreen) to the "action offstage," about which we have very sketchy information.

The principal method by which *The Blacks* moves out of the mode of play into the mode of not-play is by creating a disturbing sense of fraud or deception vis-à-vis its audience. A promise made very early in the play is found, as the play proceeds, to be quite literally kept:

ARCHIBALD (*to the audience*): This evening we shall perform for you. But, in order that you may remain comfortably settled in your seats in the presence of the drama that is *already* unfolding here, in order that you be assured that there is no danger of such a drama's worming its way into your precious lives, we shall even have the decency—a decency learned from you—to make communication impossible.

(p. 12; my emphasis)

One effect of the many "metacommunicative" remarks in the play is to bring into focus a constant *but usually carefully hidden* feature of the dramatic code: its necessary tendency to "play the world backwards."[39] Goffman's phrase, which refers to the performance of any closed, coded action, the stages and conclusion of which are known to the performers in advance, accurately describes the experience of all actors. The actors—indeed the whole crew—of a play always know exactly what is going to happen in the course of the play, and how it will all "come out." This state of complete information differs from the information states of the *spectators* (who begin with an informational vacuum) and the *characters* (who have varying degrees of information). By the end of the play, the spectators, but not necessarily the characters, attain the information states of the actors, but not necessarily of the characters; in fact, a play can be described as a communication that is completed when the receivers and senders attain informational parity.

In *The Blacks,* not only is such parity (apparently) not achieved, but constant reference is made to its lack, a lack which seems to be deliberately sought. An example of overt "backward playing" occurs when the Governor reads, from a piece of paper, a "speech" that he will have to recite (and *does* recite) later:

THE GOVERNOR (*reading more and more loudly*): "... when I fall to earth, scurvily pierced by your spears, look closely, you will behold my ascension. (*In a thundering voice*) My corpse will be on the ground, but my soul and body will rise into the air...."

(p. 13)

When harshly admonished, by another actor, to "Learn your role backstage" (p. 13), the Judge reveals the motivation for his apparent "framebreak": "That was a device to let them know that we *know*" (p. 13; my emphasis). One of the rules of the dramatic code is what has been called the *sufficiency principle,* which states that the audience always has the right amount of information about the dramatic situation.[40] At any given moment, the spectator can assume that he knows exactly as much as he needs to know in order "to follow" the drama in the way it should be followed. (Without this rule the audience of a suspense thriller would be extremely uncomfortable and might even start interrupting the play to demand more information. I have heard of experimental plays where the action is stopped to allow the audience to question the cast; however, since the actors always answer "in character," the informational disparity necessary to justify the play-process is preserved.)

The allocation of information states during a play can be tampered with only at great risk to the theatrical frame. If an actor is pushed onto stage during a play he has neither read nor rehearsed, he will not be able to perform (even if the role he is given is that of an ignoramus, a madman, or a deaf-mute) and will "break" the frame. (Another version of this is the very real actor's nightmare of "going dry" in midscene.) If an actor in character reveals information he has as an actor, a similar framebreak will result. Finally, if a spectator decided to articulate information he has about the play from a previous viewing or reading of it (for instance, if he yells to "Julius Caesar" not to go to the Forum), the resulting damage will be equally great (though very entertaining!).

The Blacks moves towards its not-play mode partly by playing havoc with conventional allocations of information states and by apparent violation of the sufficiency principle. Thus, when the Governor claims that his framebreaking "rehearsal" was a device "to let them know that we know," he is upsetting the frame of play (2) (the stage "actors"–stage "audience" interaction) by showing that it is scripted. He is asserting the "backward" construction of drama, which all actors do, but *never as characters*. When actors "play the world backwards," it is what Goffman calls "a benign fabrication,"[41] agreed upon and accepted by the "deceived" parties; when characters do it, however, it is (or, at least, it feels like) a "con." In *The Blacks*, the actors make it quite obvious that they are conning the audience, concealing vital information from them:

> ARCHIBALD: Say only what you have to. We are being watched.
>
> (pp. 28–29)

The "play" the audience is allowed to watch is consequently trivialized, regarded by one and all as a meaningless smoke screen, "scripted" not to reveal but to conceal. Even apparently crucial issues, such as the disagreement between Diouf and the others about how to relate to whites, are soon revealed as unimportant, prearranged distractions:

> ARCHIBALD: I repeat once again you're wasting your time. *We know your argument.* You're going to urge us to be reasonable, to be conciliatory.... You'll speak of love. Go right ahead, *since our speeches are set down in the script.*
>
> (p. 29; my emphasis)

Besides foregrounding the "scripted" nature of the action underway (at another point Diouf precedes an action by explaining: "Well then, I'm coming down to bury you, since that's indicated in the script"), *The Blacks* disturbs the

conventional status of its action by maintaining a curious metacommunicative discourse that thoroughly discredits the "truth" of the presented play:

> ARCHIBALD: By stretching language we'll distort it sufficiently to wrap ourselves in it and
> *hide*, whereas the masters contract it.
>
> (p. 27; my emphasis)

By such assertions, dramatic discourse, one of the principal "world-creating"
mechanisms of drama, is semiotized, its "quotation marks" made obvious, its
content reduced to lies. Language itself is rendered thoroughly problematic, a
matter of forms and oppositions rather than a referential, truth-conveying
instrument:

> ARCHIBALD: "Your *father*? Sir, don't use that word again! There was a shade of tenderness
> in your voice as you uttered it.
> VILLAGE: And what do you suggest I call *the male who knocked up the negress who gave
> birth to me?*
> ARCHIBALD: Dammit, do the best you can. Invent—if not words, then phrases that *cut you
> off rather than bind you.*
>
> (p. 26; my emphasis)

The ad hoc, constructed or semiotic nature of the language employed by
the Blacks is analogous to the semiotic—and consequently ambiguous
(because shifting)—nature of its performers:

> ARCHIBALD: But—is he still acting or is he speaking for himself?
>
> (p. 14)

The dramatic logic of the play is such that this question cannot be answered:
the actor can be acting *and* be himself, for the distinction between self and role
does not exist, or, more precisely, the self can be "played" as a role: "On this
stage, we're like guilty prisoners who play at being guilty" (p. 39). This re-
realization of identity, this assumption of the role of one's self, is reflected,
finally, in the play's destruction of physical and ontological distinctions.
"When my speech is over," says Archibald, "everything here—(he stamps his
foot in a gesture of rage) here!—will take place in the delicate world of
reprobation" (p. 12). The many ambiguities of this assertion are reminiscent of
Goffman's discussion of the problematic of situation. Archibald's speech
employs, first, a temporal marker ("When my speech is over") which turns out
to be unclear. Which speech? This one, or all the speeches that make up his
dramatic discourse? If it is the former he means, a further problem arises, for
this speech does not really end; he is interrupted, and his speech trails off in
ellipses. Secondly, what does the strongly emphasized spatial marker "here"
denote? The stage, or the "stage," or the dramatic locale? Can a dramatic place

ever be—in spite of much convincing foot-stamping—anything but virtual, not a "here" but a "there," an elsewhere? If it can, nowhere does this come closer to being the case than in *The Blacks,* and only by virtue of its relationship to the emerging structure of "real" confrontations between real blacks and real whites that the play creates. Another way of putting this is to say that the "play" performed by the blacks is not a play, but a *ritual.*

It has been common, in recent drama theory, to regard drama as a ritual, a secular ritual differing from its religious original only in the fact of referring not to a divine or supernatural order but to a human or social one. This difference, it has been noted, produces another one: ritual is *efficacious,* drama is not. The participants in a ritual do not *play* roles, they *become* other selves, and their actions as those selves are effective in, not disjunct from, the world of praxis. These actions influence the social world—by bringing rain, curing sickness, assuring a good harvest, etc.—while dramatic actions exist at a distance from the social world (even didactic plays, which seek to influence people's real lives, do not expect to do so *automatically,* but by mediation through intellect, discussion, organization, etc.).

The ritual space is, like the dramatic space, virtual rather than factual: a clearing in the woods, when designated as the locale for a ritual, becomes a holy place, bearing a spiritual potentiality it lacks in its everyday existence. (Some ritual spaces, such as temples and churches, are permanently invested with this spiritual dimension, but it is nevertheless a constructed one, capable of being "lifted"—as when, during a war, churches are used as hospitals.) However, in spite of its counterfactual status (which it shares with a dramatic space), the ritual space has a factual (practical, actual) power. The events it encloses are *not* fictional, but "real" (at least for its participants), bearing a real, *causal* relationship to events outside.

The assumed causal relationship between ritual and social worlds obtains in the play performed by the Blacks (play (5)) as well as in the macroplay. The murder of the white woman is pure ritual: the reenactment of a prior event that releases the same spiritual and psychological meanings as the original. In semiotic terms, it is a psychological (though not physical) *double* of the original crime, for it entails all the hatred, resentment, violence, cruelty, fear and ambiguity of the first one:

> SNOW: If I were sure that Village bumped the woman off in order to heighten the fact that he's a scarred, smelly, thick-lipped, snub-nosed negro, an eater and guzzler of Whites and all other colors, a drooling, sweating, belching, spitting, coughing, farting goat-fucker, a licker of white boots, a good-for-nothing, sick, oozing oil and sweat, limp and submissive, if I were sure he killed her in order to merge with the night . . . but I know he loved her.
>
> (p. 27)

But, it will be objected, there *is* no original, the murder committed by Village before the play began is part of the macroplay's fiction, coded diegetically. This is true in fact, but not in effect. The play's use of real blacks and real whites (the audience) forces an extradramatic context into existence, one in which a crime of the sort Village commits is not a fiction but a fact, recorded in countless newspapers.

In the same way, the macroplay is a psychological double of actual social reality, containing all the role-playing, fraud, deceit, contempt and threat of its real counterpart. The white woman's "death wasn't meant to signify merely that she lost her life." Its signification unfolds onstage, as the ritual is performed, but "the ultimate gesture is performed off-stage."

The Architecture of Emptiness

An Arab's an Arab.

Sir Harold, in *The Screens*

In the radically deconstructive context of Genet's drama, an assertion of absolute identity of the sort Sir Harold indulges in is the epitome of delusion. If there is one idea that underlies and sums up the theatrical experience of his plays, it is that all identities are constructed and hence problematic. They are temporary, arbitrary, and unstable correlations between signifiers and signifieds; their existence depends upon the operation of a code: they are, in short, *signs*. In this context an Arab is no more (eternally and profoundly) an Arab than a black is a black, a bishop a bishop, or a brothel a brothel. The nostalgia for enduring identity that Sir Harold's remark evinces is a denial of context, of semiosis, of history. Yet it is itself the product of a historical moment and the badge of a social class. It belongs to those given over, blindly, to what Roland Barthes termed "the petit-bourgeois predilection for tautological reasoning."[1] It is the climax of nineteenth-century positivism and the last desperate refusal of relativism.

Positivism, which inscribed its conviction of certainty in the structure of the universal positive proposition—"this is so"—has crumbled, and its demise is recorded in the structure of tautology, of the universal proposition folding back upon itself: "this is this." This collapse can be explained, as Richard Coe indicates, in sociohistorical terms: "But since the days of Pisarev, much has changed, and above all, our reaction to those who proclaim what they choose to announce as being the Truth. The Word of God has become the verbiage of mass-communication, the shining weapon of Truth has become the ingenious trickery of publicity and propaganda. . . . For us, the positive, all-embracing truth or injunction is tainted with the corruption of uncertainty. We live, argued Nathalie Sarraute, in an era of *suspicion*" (emphasis in original).[2] There is a puzzling negative value judgment in Coe's phrase "the corruption of uncertainty"—puzzling in the light of his recognition, a few lines later, of the power of analyses that are based on a recognition of uncertainty: "That truth—if such a thing exists at all—lies, not in the conventional formulae of assertion, but in the dynamic forces that may be generated by negation, is the discovery, the vital and guiding principle, of the Existentialist generation."[3] In Coe's formulation there lurks the suggestion that, having lost the paradise of certainty, we are condemned to search for it by circuitous means. But to regard it thus may be finally to harbor, in a more complex form, Sir Harold's brand of positivist nostalgia. It is not until the very notion of certainty—and not just of its possibility—is abandoned altogether that the curtain finally falls on positivism.

Meanwhile, the desire for coherence and plenitude of existence is satisfied by tautology, by a militant proclamation of identity which masks, as Barthes argues, a cowardly retreat from analysis:

> We understand at least what such vacuity in definition affords those who brandish it so proudly: a kind of minor ethical salvation, the satisfaction of having militated in favor of truth... without having to assume the risks which any somewhat positive search for the truth inevitably involves: tautology dispenses us from having ideas, but at the same time prides itself on making this license into a stern morality; whence its success: laziness is promoted to the rank of rigor. Racine is Racine: admirable security of nothingness.[4]

It is all such security, all such pursuits of positive truths which fail to assume their inherent risks, that Genet's dramaturgy attacks and undermines.

This attack, to which a philosophical (ethical and epistemological) character can be assigned (following Barthes), is carried out by Genet in the *theatrical* realm, and takes the form of an "analysis" or deconstruction of theatrical signs and codes. For example, if Genet's point about positivist delusions had been made simply by a satirical treatment of characters (like Sir Harold) who suffer from them, Genet would himself have been implicated in the same erroneous thinking. By equating a character with an intellectual or ideological position, he would be following the pattern of symbolic "thesis" plays, and turning his theater into a mere vehicle for an idea that exists independently of, and prior to, its performance. His theater would be, then, a discursive theater, tacitly accepting the unselfconscious code of realistic drama: this actor *is* this character; "this is so."

Yet this very operation, this equating of a character with a position, be it philosophical, moral, or political, is the cornerstone of all thematic criticism of Genet's plays. I have already discussed its presence in readings influenced by Sartre and noted its inevitable discovery of author-surrogates in the plays. Even Bernard Dort, who begins by explicitly rejecting the Sartrian tradition (saying that, in the last three plays, written after the publication of Sartre's study, "Genet the writer detached himself, thanks to Sartrian mediation, from

Genet the character"),[5] nevertheless cannot resist finding Genet the character again in *The Balcony*: "This double character [the beggar/slave]...doubtless represents the poet, indeed Genet himself."[6]

Political interpretations of Genet's plays perform the same operation of turning a character into a symbol. Lucien Goldmann, even though in general insisting that art and reality are "homologous" only at the level of "mental structures" or "categories,"[7] nevertheless equates characters with positions ("Kadidja...is the incarnation of the village," "Ommu...incarnates the expectations of the village," etc.).[8] He offers psychological explanations for the characters' actions (for example, Roger castrates himself in "despair"),[9] a process which belongs to a mode of interpretation precisely contrary to that required by a writer who insists: "I have never copied life—an event or a man, the Algerian war or colonialists."[10] Goldmann's method of analysis yields a beautifully coherent reading of the plays. It makes of *The Screens,* for example, a lucid political statement: "The Action is divided into four stages, representing both society's development and Saïd's increasingly radical attitudes."[11] To the comfort of this description I must oppose Genet's own statement: "People say that plays are generally supposed to have a meaning: not this one. It is a celebration whose elements are disparate. It is a celebration of nothing."[12]

Although Goldmann's reading acknowledges the importance of "nothing" in the play, it gives that "nothing" a political character: "Nothingness" is the fourth "stage" of the play's action, the one to which Saïd escapes "direct"[13] and in so doing goes beyond the danger of participating in a new, revolutionary but potentially repressive political order. Thus, far from rising to Genet's claim that his play has no meaning, Goldmann ascribes to it a very clear and coherently developed—discursive—message.

Of course, Genet's claims are of no significance to the sociologist, who begins with the premise that the "mental structures" of art have nothing to do with "the writer's conscious intentions or hidden motives."[14] Besides being contradicted by Goldmann's readings of the plays (where intentionality is implicitly acknowledged), this denial of conscious intention to the author is, in my view, an ideological move of a rather authoritarian sort. In finding an author duplicating, willy-nilly, the concerns of his age, the critic is not far from those who, following Sartre, find Genet reenacting, willy-nilly, the rape of his identity by a word-wielding and repressive society. Pursued to their logical extremes, which Goldmann does not do, both approaches reduce the plays to "documents"—psychological and political case studies. The result: we discover a brutalized neurotic or an intellectual rebel, cowering desperately behind his supposedly "artistic" gestures.

I do not mean to belittle Goldmann's analysis, which is brilliant. Yet its brilliance, which lies in its lucidity, may be the very thing that ultimately misrepresents Genet, ascribing to his work an intellectual coherence and thereby "naturalizing" or "normalizing" it. Perhaps such "normalizing" is inevitable, dictated by the discursive mode of literary criticism, which is in the business of paraphrasing, of renaming to render "intelligible." It may well be that in the case of a writer like Genet, whose plays appear to pursue self-erasure through contradiction and confusion, any "reading" will misrepresent the experience of the plays, merely reinscribing the various "stages" through which the plays pass and which they successively deconstruct and deny. Since it is precisely the naming of things—the "construction" of reality through semiosis—that Genet's plays expose, all "naming" after the fact (which is what criticism is) becomes implicated in his denial.

This is precisely where Genet differs from Brecht. Whereas the latter creates a drama that points towards—and enjoins—critical thinking, a drama that encourages renaming and sees it as a way to get at social truth and political reality, Genet's drama defeats critical thinking, allowing it to proceed only in constant self-denial and self-erasure. Goldmann claims that Genet's plays "have overall a realistic and *didactic* [in the Brechtian sense of the word] structure."[15] His claim that *The Balcony*'s "subject, perfectly clear, almost *didactic*, is, as a matter of fact, constituted by the essential transformations of the industrial society in the first half of the century"[16] makes of the play, as Dort says, "a vast realistic parable."[17]

There are many reasons for avoiding such a conclusion. Firstly, there are Genet's own numerous assertions of apoliticality. Even about *The Maids* (which, along with *Deathwatch,* seems to me to be a fairly discursive play of ideas) he tries to shift the focus away from political and sociological matters: "One thing must be written: this has nothing to do with an argument on the lot of domestics. I suppose servants have their unions—that's no business of ours."[18] (It is important to notice that Genet's statement about his play is phrased negatively; he tells us what it is not, not what it is.) A similar disavowal of political motives accompanies *The Blacks*: "If my plays help Blacks, I do not worry about it. I don't believe it, however. I believe that action, the direct fight against colonialism, does more for Blacks than a play."[19] Perhaps Genet's most powerful antididactic statement is the famous one made about *The Balcony*: "One more thing: this play should not be performed as if it were a satire of this or that. It is—and will therefore be performed as—the glorification of the Image and of the Reflection. Its meaning—satirical or not—will only appear in this way."[20] The most striking thing about Genet's comments on his plays is that they are always about their *performance*. On the "meanings" of his plays Genet is always silent— permitting himself only to say what they are *not* about. Of course, this cannnot automatically be translated into an injunction against interpretation. Indeed it might be argued that Genet's interpretive silence is precisely the reason for critics to redouble their interpretive efforts. However, such an effort should at least take into account what Genet says, instead of ignoring it altogether.

Genet's insistence on performance can lead to an identification of his theatrical practice with the theory that stands at the opposite extreme from Brecht's: Artaud's. Indeed, Genet has been read as playing Sophocles to Artaud's Aristotle. But, as Bernard Dort convincingly argues, Genet is far from Artaud's dream of bringing the true forces of life onto the stage. It is not unmediated "life" born of spontaneous, unrehearsed, and presemiotic gestures that Genet's theater creates, but the very opposite: mediation and semiosis itself: the endless play of difference. "It is less the body which Genet wants to expose on stage than its disguises. . . . While [Artaud] takes exception to rehearsal, in that it is repetition, diminution, and disguise, Genet makes it the very object of his theater; he stages and exalts it."[21]

Thus we see that the attempt to characterize Genet's dramaturgy resembles that dramaturgy in one crucial respect: it adopts a rhetoric of rejection. Genet is not Brecht; Genet is not Artaud. Nor is he Pirandello, for his "celebration" of Appearance, which I have described as his analysis of signification, does not, like Pirandello's, identify appearance with "an essential truth which people do not manage either to articulate or to live in their day-to-day existence but which they can grasp in the practice of drama."[22] Genet's drama gives us nothing to "grasp," that is, to name.

Genet's drama enacts the deconstruction of such notions as reality and identity, integrating this analysis into every aspect of the plays, including staging and acting. In so doing, he creates a drama that belongs to, or at least moves towards, a time beyond what Heidegger called *Die Zeit des Weltbildes*: the time of the world as picture. This new time is characterized by a new mode of perception, one that is multiple and mobile instead of single and static. It dispenses with the separate, onlooking *viewpoint,* and assumes instead a fluid, unstable, and indefinable *experience*. No longer the world as picture, this is now the world as signification, ceaseless and inconclusive.

Some critics have recognized the similarity between this mode of perception and that of the ancient East: "In the past, it was the East which based its philosophy on the dynamic negative, the inconceivable, the plenum void; the West preferred its lucid concepts, its clear and distinct ideas, its positive logic, its logical positivism."[23] However, to the extent that Genet's drama is primarily a theatrical drama rather than a philosophical one, it may be closer to the physicality of primitive rituals than to the spirituality of Tao or Zen. He himself hints at this, in a characteristically vague and allusive way: "I have no idea what the drama will be like in a socialist world: I have a much better notion what it would be like under the Mau-Mau."[24]

Genet, then, is not Brecht, not Artaud, not Pirandello, not Lao Tsu. He cannot easily be placed in a theoretical niche. We might wish to overcome this failure of classification by asserting that "Genet is Genet," but to do so would be, of course, to succumb to Sir Harold's cognitive disease. Perhaps, recalling the mode of writing under erasure which I have identified as characteristic of Genet's dramaturgy, we might get away with saying that Genet is G~~e~~net. However, we are really interested in his plays, and about their structure and functioning it is possible to say a few things.

Theater and Difference: An Overview of Genet's Practice

What do you mean far away? It's behind the screen.
Virtue, in *The Blacks*

As I have shown, contradiction and confusion inform Genet's plays—to such an extent that, together, they constitute his dramatic method. This method is, I believe, so pervasive, so active at all theoretical levels, that it cannot be fully or accurately described in the literary (language-oriented) terms of traditional drama criticism.

The semiotics of theater not only provides a set of terms and concepts capable of following and capturing Genet's practice more effectively, but also, because of the metasemiotic nature of Genet's practice, is itself clarified and specified by an analysis of that practice. This double focus, which I have tried to maintain throughout this study, reveals that Genet's drama is an exploration of two major sign systems—space and actors—and the various codes pertaining to them. Each of these sign systems comprises several others (see figure 1), about all of which Genet's drama makes some metasemiotic points (i.e., which it puts under analysis). This analysis has the following effects:

1. In working with the difference between signifiers and signifieds (e.g., actors-characters, stage-place, costumes-clothes, even words-things) Genet opens up a space of *emptiness,* a void which can only be characterized by what it is *not,* and which gradually engulfs the whole play.
2. Genet's major technique for creating this emptiness is by situating his drama at *boundaries* of various sorts (costume, skin, masks, veils, curtains, screens). It is not at all surprising that Genet's last play is entitled *The Screens,* and critics may be missing an important point in thinking that "*The Screens* is the only work by Genet whose title refers to its form and not to its content."[25] Moreover, these boundaries are always fragile, vulnerable. Again, it is entirely appropriate that one of the climactic moments of the final play is the rupture of, and passage through, a paper screen (p. 143).

Figure 1

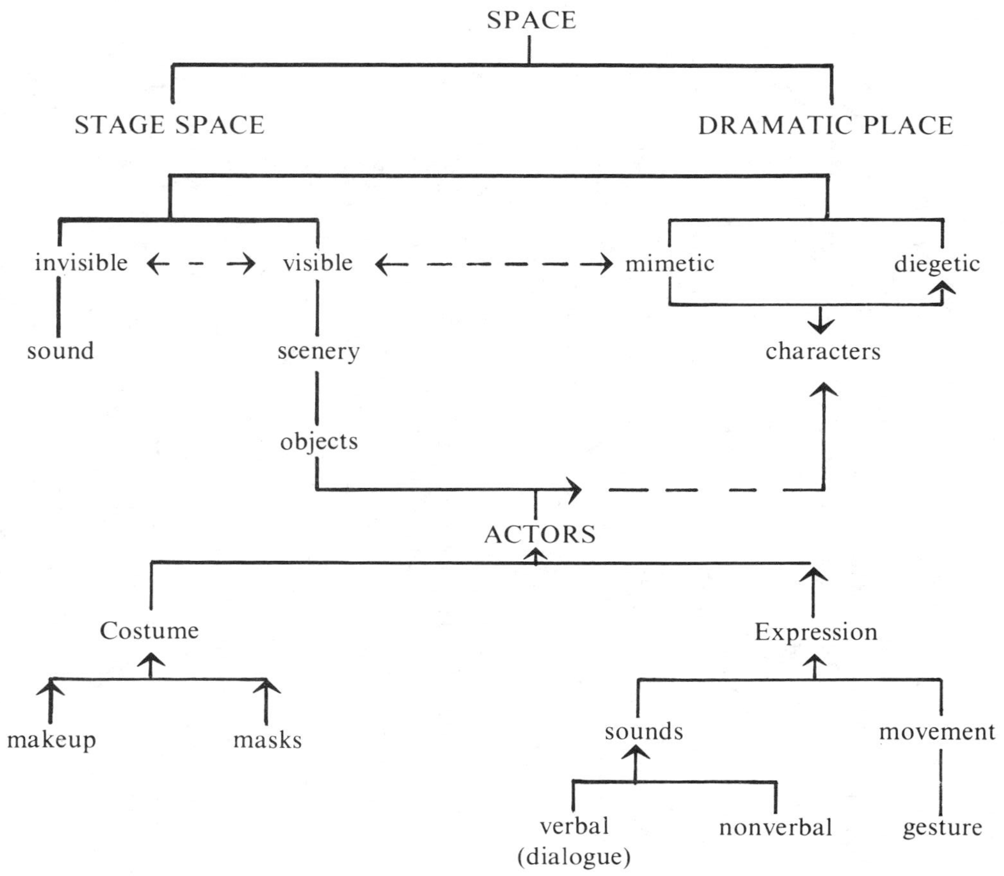

SPACE

STAGE SPACE   DRAMATIC PLACE

invisible ← — → visible — — → mimetic   diegetic

sound   scenery   characters

               objects

ACTORS

Costume   Expression

makeup   masks   sounds   movement

                          verbal   nonverbal   gesture
                        (dialogue)

Archibald's phrase, "the architecture of emptiness," captures the overall form and content of Genet's plays. It is a process that begins by deconstructing theatrical spaces, proceeds to deconstruct a variety of other sign systems (actors, costumes, gesture, language), and ends by creating emptiness, which is to say: by erasing the stage.

Space

A play involves two primary kinds of space: actual (real, theatrical: *stage space*) and virtual (fictional, dramatic: *dramatic place*).[26] The former, stage space, can be of two sorts, visible and nonvisible—nonvisible space being constituted by offstage sound (the acoustic (off)stage). The fictional space of a play—dramatic place—can also be divided into two types: mimetic space and diegetic space. Mimetic space is that fictional place or places that can be directly represented on stage: it is the signified of the stage-space signifier. To put it differently, mimetic space is the space of that part of the fiction that can be presented within the audience's evidential boundaries (on the visible stage space and the acoustic (off)stage space). Diegetic space, on the other hand, is the space of that part of the fiction which is *described,* through narration, by the characters. The audience's access to it is mediated by the mimetic part of the fiction; it is consequently, one might say, a fiction's fiction.

Mimetic space and diegetic space. The relationship between the mimetic and diegetic spaces of a play is mutually supportive. At least, it is so in realistic drama, a feature of the code of that drama that avant-garde drama often works against. Beckett's plays, for instance, use diegetic spaces but render them problematic. Indeed, *Waiting for Godot* can be read entirely as a drama of diegetic failure: everything about Godot, including his very identity, is presented nonmimetically, and the diegetic mentions of him are fraught with uncertainty.

Genet's method is a little different. It is not that he privileges the mimetic level of his plays, as Beckett does, over the diegetic, but that he relates the two in contradictory, mutually effacing ways. Thus, instead of creating a drama frozen inescapably onto the stage space—like Beckett's—he creates a drama that denies reality to both the mimetic and to the diegetic spaces. In this way he erases the stage, replacing it with emptiness.

The paradox of the offstage gesture, discussed in the preceding chapter, is a striking example of contradictory correlation of these two kinds of dramatic space. The space to which Village "goes" is first *described* at length and in detail, diegetically created and defined as "far away":

> BOBO: ... But at the same time they've got to go elsewhere. They have to cross the room, go through the garden, take a path lined with hazel trees, turn left, push aside the thorns, throw salt in front of them, put on boots, enter the woods....
>
> (p. 83)

However, this diegetic space has already, and through the same means (dialogue), been established as being, simply, "behind the screen." In short, diegetic space is brought very close to being a part of mimetic space, a part of the acoustic (off)stage.

It is worth reiterating what the overall effect of such undermining is. To deny the truth of a play's diegetic space is to threaten the play's fictional world: the very world, it must be remembered, upon which plays traditionally depend for their unity of meaning.[27] It is also, in effect, to deny the play's traditional status as a sincere, code-abiding activity, part of an enterprise linking two sympathetic, mutually supportive groups: performers and spectators.

Mimetic space and stage space. Genet's disruption of traditional theater-space codes is not restricted to the mimetic and diegetic codes. In *The Balcony,* as we saw, the mimetic space itself is full of contradictions and confusions, the result of a rupture between the scenic realm (signifier) and the dramatic one (signified). Thus the "center" of the allegedly central Mausoleum Studio turns out to be an "antechamber"; the other studios appear to be both the same and different; and the relationship between the world of the play and the world of the audience is both continuous and disjunct. (The mirror in the studios reflects a bed that would logically be, but is not, in the first rows of the auditorium.)

An equally contradictory version of mimetic space exists in *The Screens,* where the spatial realms of the dead and the living are correlated in two mutually contradictory ways. In scene 15, stage space is organized so that the space of the dead is on the ground floor (i.e., below), while that of the living is on the second floor (i.e., above). This spatial relationship is, however, contradicted by the scene's gestural signification, for when an action occurs on the second floor (i.e., above) *"All the dead lower their heads [to observe it] although the mother [alive] is above them."*[28] The scene incorporates a denial of an aspect of the theatrical code hitherto taken for granted: the simultaneous and supportive deployment of several signs belonging to different sign systems. Here, two signs—spatial organization and gesture—which ordinarily reinforce one another (and in so doing disguise their individual constructed ("sign") natures) are used in a disjunct, contradictory way. The result is a heightening of artificiality and a loss of coherence. This effect, it seems to me, gets in the way of an interpretation like Goldmann's, which depends on finding a coherent system of relationships between the living and the dead.

Visible and nonvisible mimetic space. Mimetic space, as I have mentioned, is that part of the fiction which is directly presented to the audience, existing within its evidential boundaries. These boundaries are of two kinds: visual and aural. The relationship between the two is yet another traditionally stable one that Genet subverts. Usually, what offstage acoustic signs constitute for any given scene is a supposedly contiguous mimetic space that remains *constant* for the duration of the scene and is also taken to exist in all other instances of the visible space's use in the play. For example, the voices of Regina and Osvald at the end of act 1 of Ibsen's *Ghosts,* along with "the sound of a chair knocked over,"[29] constitute an offstage mimetic space—//the dining room//—which can be assumed to be offstage in all succeeding scenes set in this front room.

Genet breaks this rule frequently. In *The Balcony,* a woman's scream is heard offstage and initially serves to define the offstage space as a mimetic space—another studio. However, the second instance of the scream is more problematic: it does not sound, as the Bishop says, like "a make-believe scream," and Irma is not sure either. In this way Genet changes—or puts into question—the referent of this acoustic sign: does it stand for an //actress-prostitute// playing a role for a sadistic client in another studio? Or for a //real woman// screaming—and, if the latter is the case, is she in a studio or outside the brothel? Besides offering conflicting nonvisible mimetic spaces (i.e., //a neighboring studio// vs. //a street//) this acoustic sign also forces the very nature of acoustic signs into the audience's consciousness. For, in the theater, every scream *is* a "make-believe scream," and every space it constitutes is, first and foremost, *theatrical* space.

The Blacks incorporates another kind of disruption of the "visible-nonvisible mimetic space" opposition. As I have shown in the preceding chapter, the central and paradoxical mode of the play is "displayed concealment," a paradox captured beautifully in Felicity's promise that "Before long you'll see what's hidden behind our display" (p. 106). What is "hidden," of course, is the trial and execution, backstage, of a renegade Negro. This execution occurs in a nonvisible mimetic space constituted by the *"sound of a firecracker"* (p. 109) but literally explodes into the visible space: *"The sparks of the fireworks are seen against the black velvet set."* Genet's insistence on this willful "explosion" of the fiction, his exposure of the acoustic signifiers as signifying not //bullets// but //firecrackers//, is puzzling. It would seem at first glance to undermine the mode of "actual threat" I have ascribed to the play. However, a closer analysis reveals that it is not an abandoning of the "real" action level (microplay (6)) but a final completion of its "hidden" status. The discursive signification of the visible fireworks is as follows: "We are denying you even acoustic access to the really important event. You had thought you would at least hear it take place, but what you are hearing is a fake version of it, not the real thing."

Finally, in *The Screens,* (off)stage mimetic space is also revealed to be theatrical, but by a process that is the reverse of the one in *The Blacks.* Here, instead of moving a sign from a dramatic signification to a theatrical one,

Genet does the opposite. The offstage "barnyard" constituted by "animal sounds" is predefined as "fake" by a "rehearsal" of those sounds by Leila:

> THE MOTHER: I want a barnyard around us. And I want it to come out of our bellies. Can you do the rooster?
> LEILA (*intently*): Cock . . . cock . . . cock-a-doodle-doo!
> THE MOTHER (*angrily*): That's a damaged rooster. I won't have it! Do it again.
> LEILA (*in a vibrant voice*): Cock-a-doodle-doo!
>
> (p. 27)

Thus, when, a few minutes later, we hear /barnyard sounds/ offstage, they signify not //animals// but //Leila making animal sounds//. Whereas in the earlier examples, it was a case of the fiction exploding onto the stage and becoming defictionalized, here the stage moves into the wings, defictionalizing the (off)stage.

Scenery. Any attempt to situate Genet's scenic practice in the recent history of the stage encounters as many obstacles as does the attempt to situate his dramaturgic practice in that tradition. In a discussion of Genet's décors, as in speaking of his dramatic method, a rhetoric of negation arises. His stage is of course not realistic, yet it does not easily fit into any of the categories of non- or antirealistic staging techniques. It is not symbolic, not expressionistic, not constructivist, not surrealistic, not epic—although it shares certain features with all of these, especially the last two. Like the surrealists, Genet incorporates everyday objects into his décor in nonrealistic ways. Like Brecht, he foregrounds the theatrical, artificial nature of his décor. However, whereas Brecht "undresses" the stage, using only a few carefully selected, simple, and functional (as opposed to decorative and illusionistic) elements, Genet "dresses up" his stage, making it visually rich (color, images) and materially opulent (velvet, lace, chandeliers).

Both this similarity and this difference to Brecht's practice are particularly evident in *The Screens,* where the décor (which is the drama) explodes with colors and images, but never ceases to declare its flimsy and constructed nature, being entirely dependent on the moveable screens.

One reason for this visual richness may be syntactical: it contrasts powerfully with the stage's emptiness in the play's final moments. *The Screens* ends on a bare stage, from which even the plain white screens of the dead have been removed by the departing actors. *"The stage is empty,"* Genet writes (p. 201). This emptiness, all the more empty by contrast to the fullness created throughout by the colorful screens, is like the emptiness of the Mother's valise, or the emptiness of the catafalque in *The Blacks*: the mark of betrayal, the exposure of a lie. The bare stage at the end of *The Screens,* which has often been interpreted as a positive Absence, a free space beyond signification and appearance, is, in its *effect,* nothing positive. Far from providing the sense of a completion or closure that such an interpretation implies, it creates a sense of loss, of theatrical withdrawal. As such, it is similar to the conclusion of *The Balcony* and *The Blacks,* both of which end by asserting a *continuation* from which the audience is excluded. To turn Genet's "vide" into an image of completion or resolution is to neutralize his drama of denial, which denies closure itself.

I have said that the screens *are* the drama. This is revealed in the uses to which they are put. Besides defining places (= set function) and symbolizing the difference between two states of consciousness (living and dead), they are also, and most importantly, the *loci* of action. They are, in fact, used as a kind of second-order stage, upon which the characters inscribe their acts. (Significantly, it is the Arabs who use them in this way.) In scene 10, they set fire to an orange grove, an action that occurs entirely on the surface of the screens. Entering one at a time, armed with chalk, they draw flames *"at the foot of each orange tree"*; one *"blows on the fire"*; one *"stirs it with his hand"* (pp. 71–75).

All this takes place behind the backs (literally) of the orchard owners, who are "animatedly" *talking.* Significantly, their talk brings them, finally, to a discussion of *language.* Taken together, these two actions bring into being a complex and powerful paradox: the *creation,* in silence, of *destruction,* in the shadow of language. While Sir Harold and Mr. Blankensee congratulate themselves that their superiority is unquestionable, because "we're the lords of language" (p. 74), their "real" power (property) is "destroyed" by wordless images.

The meaning of this scene emerges fully in contrast to scene 13, where the screens are once again used as surfaces. Here, however, they prove to be surfaces of projection and passivity instead of realization and action. The French Lieutenant uses the screen in a way that parodies a military leader's use of a map or blackboard to plot out a campaign. The screen becomes not a place but a diagram, a reduction of reality corresponding, in importance, to the French army's desperate attempts to keep their power. As a mere diegetic aid, the screen falls far short of its potential power (realized by the Arabs). Whereas the Arabs achieve destruction through images, the French make images lamely follow after words, illustrating ideas and hopes instead of embodying them.

Objects. Objects, being primarily visual signs, pose special problems for semiotic theory. Of all theatrical signs they seem to be the ones most given to importing their extratheatrical connotations directly into the theatrical realm. Yet, as has long been recognized, "the adaptation of objects...to the specifically theatrical code involves a process of recodification."[30] An object on stage becomes, in Petr Bogatyrev's famous formulation, "sign of a sign and not sign of an object."[31]

Recent studies of the use of objects in avant-garde theater show the presence of a conscious effort at "resemanticization"[32] of objects, often with disastrous effects on the plays' communicational power. Both Brecht and Grotowski, it has been noted, expose "the intra- and extratheatrical 'contracts' on which the traditional and fixed identity of objects is based as flimsy, relative and changeable."[33] However, such exposure is often ideologically motivated; it is implicitly an attack on the iconic objects of the naturalistic theater, which "is identified with material well-being, wastefulness (witness the sums it spends on the construction of the true-to-life setting), a lack of imagination, and of course a 'bourgeois-capitalist' ideology."[34] This use of objects—or "semioticized objects"—often proves to be too complex for the ordinary spectator:

> Unfortunately, both extreme resemanticization of objects and the twofold ideological context to which it is related often remain beyond the grasp of the spectator, creating thereby a communicational gap between the theater and its audience. . . . The spectator may even fail to recognize the ideological dimension of a particularly original or esoteric resemanticization, because he is likely to ignore the history of the theater and its techniques in the nineteenth and twentieth centuries, knowledge essential for the attribution of the resemanticized object to any semantic field.[35]

An initial example of Genet's use of objects will show how he manages to avoid this problem. In scene 9 of *The Screens,* Leila is seen talking to various familiar objects. Already, resemanticization has begun, because the action is, by extratheatrical codes, "ungrammatical": people, not objects, are listeners in everyday discourse. Furthermore, Leila's speech and actions explicitly bring together two semantic fields to which the object is related, the first being extratheatrical, the second not:

> LEILA (*to a cheese grater*): You won't have much to do, we never put cheese into the noodles. . . . To keep you busy I'll scrape the callus on the sole of my foot.
>
> (p. 61)

What Leila's manipulation does—and this is typical of Genet's treatment of all signs—is that instead of losing one connotation (the social one) altogether, it keeps it active alongside the new, idiosyncratic one. The cheese grater, acquiring *two* functions, becomes a potentiality without ceasing to manifest its identity. We see it, therefore, both as a thing (or, more precisely, as a social sign) and as a (theatrical) sign.

Perhaps Genet's finest dramatization of the semiotic nature of objects occurs in the photographer scene in *The Balcony,* where two objects—a *"rolled up sheet of paper"*and *"a monocle"*—are transformed, for the purpose of completing the portraits of the General and the Bishop, into *"a marshall's baton"* and *"a Host"* (p. 74). The action dramatizes the process of resemanticizing itself. Most critics have interpreted this scene as a satire or celebration of Appearance, a gloss on the idea with which it concludes: "It is a true image, born of a false spectacle." It is that, but perhaps its full significance emerges when proper attention is paid to the *terms*—the objects—in question.

The sheet of paper belongs to the (extratheatrical) semantic field "writing." It is a surface of inscription, upon which a language is frozen or captured. The connotations of this field would be: the "written word," "decrees," "laws," *"power."* Resemanticized as "a marshall's baton" it belongs to the semantic field "symbol of military rank," with the connotations "hierarchy," "repression," "violence," *"power."* The resemanticization thus involves in fact a mere *translation,* from one kind of power to another. This translation is, however, in the direction of actualization, an un-translation in fact, a recovery of the original form of power before it became "coded." (This direction is reflected in the direction of the morphological change from surface (paper) to substance (wood: the source of paper).)

The second object, the monocle, begins in the semantic field "sight" and has the connotations "perception" (but also "blindness": hence, "artificially aided perception"), "observation," "knowledge," "power," as well as the connotation "fascism" (the monocle is a common attribute of the popular image of a Nazi commander and here belongs to the General). In its resemanticized version, as Host, it belongs to the semantic field "Christianity"—specifically "Catholicism"—and has the connotations "hierarchy," "authority," "mystery." Here, then, the resemanticization translates from one kind of vision to another, and by a process isomorphic to that seen in the first case, redefines religion as artificial sight, myopia. It is within the interplay of these semantic fields that the significance of the words "true image" and "false spectacle" is released.

Genet's objects, then, are resemanticized in such a way that they deconstruct signification *and* expose its underlying ideology, but do not lose the audience in the process. The reason for this is that, unlike Brecht's and Grotowski's, Genet's resemanticization is not at the service of another ideology which will only be satisfied when it has annihilated the old significance and replaced it with a new one. It is the simultaneous entertaining of two signifieds that is Genet's method, not the privileging of one or the other.

The postmodernism of Genet's plays involves another unusual treatment of objects: the transformation, *into* objects, of signs from other sign systems. This phenomenon, which I have earlier called the objective imperative, takes us into the second major sign system (see figure 1) that Genet's dramaturgy puts under analysis.

Actors

Genet's use of the actor-character sign involves exposure of an aspect of the dramatic code that I have not mentioned explicitly before: namely, the multiplicity of its communication levels. Whole theatrical messages are conveyed by a superimposition of various *kinds* of messages occurring between various communicating entities: actors and actors, actors and spectators, characters and spectators, characters and characters, a director and actors, a director and spectators.[36]

A play like *The Blacks* proceeds precisely by confusing these various levels, so much so that many utterances resist decoding because the identity of their "addresser" and "addressees" is uncertain. Archibald's many directions to the Negroes can be taken to be communications occurring either between actor and actors, or character and characters, or actor and spectators.

Moreover, the actor aspect of Genet's characters is always stressed, frequently by shifts in tone (from natural to artificial) but also by assumption of costumes, comments on roles, etc. An extreme case of this is Diouf in *The Blacks*, who becomes the signifier for various character signifieds (as does Arthur in *The Balcony*). In *The Screens*, actors often split themselves off temporarily from their characterological functions to assume nonhuman signifieds: Leila and the Mother become animals, Saïd and Habib become the wind (p. 34). (Both instances echo the Blacks' imitation of the "African jungle" (p. 12).)

But perhaps the most important method of actor-objectification in Genet's plays is the transformation of characters into *mirrors* for each other. In *The Balcony*, success in experiencing the self is predicated on this transformation, and failure is defined as *"being"* (instead of *"becoming"*) one's image. The French army in *The Screens* appears to suffer from another kind of failure, that of trying—but not succeeding—to become mirrors. The Lieutenant (whose dependence on words and consequent impotence were dramatized in his parodic use of the screen as map) proclaims the need for mutual reflection ("Let every man be a mirror of every other man" (p. 119)), but to no avail: his discourse ends in fragmentation instead of self-realization: "A curl in the curl opposite; the heart in the heart opposite; the foot in the foot; the nose in the nose; the foot in the nose; the eye in the teeth" (p. 120).

Costume. Genet's "architecture of emptiness" depends upon the dramatic use of a quasi-topographic opposition: empty-full. The opposition focuses attention on the boundaries of things, boundaries which constitute emptiness as fullness (e.g., the cloth over the nonexistent catafalque, the cardboard of the empty valise). One of the most powerful of these constituting surfaces is costume, which, in Genet's plays, ranks with the mirror in constitutive power.

Like the mirror, it can trap one into an inauthentic, static experience of the self. This occurs when it becomes the self, instead of being the channel through and across which the self flows. This appears to have happened to Mr. Blankensee, who wears a pad on his stomach and back because "A man of my age who doesn't have a belly and ass hasn't much prestige. So one has to fake a little" (p. 73).

In contrast to Mr. Blankensee, who pads himself up to give an appearance of fullness, the Arabs use costume to empty themselves, not to display but to hide. There is Leila, hooded throughout the play, and Warda, who is all exterior: "My outfits! Underneath, there's not much left" (p. 22). Her emptiness is carefully concealed by a deceptively "heavy" surface (just like the deceptively heavy suitcase):

> WARDA (*counting her bracelets*): There's one missing. You'll bring it in. *I have to be heavy.* . . . A bracelet missing! As if I were a coffin and a hammer stroke missing.
>
> (p. 18; my emphasis)

The analogy between self and coffin (we are reminded of the missing catafalque) proves to be apt, and is driven home by repeated comparisons between the self and a vessel, closed, hollow space—the nothingness into which power spends itself: "This is the brothel," says Malika, where "men empty themselves" (p. 21).

In *The Screens,* emptiness, disguised by deceptive exteriors, is a political weapon. The mask or veil organizes revolt:

> GENDARME: Moslem women! I know your tricks all right! One day . . . one carnival day with a sheet and a rag I disguised myself as an Arab woman, a Fatima. All at once, straight off, I grasped your mentality. Caught on in a flash. And if circumstances force me, in spite of my wound and my two daughters, I'll take the veil again.
>
> (pp. 67–68)

The veil is to self what the screen is to reality in this play: the mark of a fiction, the sign of an absent, static identity.

It is precisely in its existence on the presence-absence axis that the power of costume lies, as is dramatized when a costume detaches itself from its social function (= clothes) and becomes an object. In scene 3, Leila dances around, and addresses *"a pair of worn, patched trousers . . . which is standing upright towards the left side of the stage"* (p. 24). The objectification of this costume turns out to be a first step towards a more important transformation—of costume into character:

> THE MOTHER: . . . If he lays out his pants for the night, it's they who keep watch on a chair, it's they who guard you and frighten you. . . . Saïd can doze away. He knows that pants have to live, and it's the patches that keep them on their toes, and the liveliest are those that are inside out.
>
> (p. 26)

In a later scene, another costume sign is transformed into an object sign: *"A wonderful pigskin glove flies in, directed by a mechanism behind the screen. It remains in the air, as if suspended, in the center of the stage"* (p. 32). This glove, which belongs to Sir Harold and which he used as an accessory to his authority (*"Whenever he is on stage, he plays a great deal with his glove and whip"* (p. 40)), achieves its full power when it is detached from him, when it is pure costume:

SAÏD: Good God! What's in it? His fist?
HABIB: Straw. Packed tight, so as to look as if his fist were in.... And so as to look more
    dangerous... And to look more real....
SAÏD: It looks more beautiful.

(pp. 32–33)

It is as sign, detached from its function but still nevertheless recalling it, that costume completes its significance in Genet's plays: both full and empty, it is another instance of the "structure" of "emptiness."

Language. The complete version of the phrase of Archibald that I have borrowed is: "an architecture of emptiness *and words.*" Traditional Genet criticism, focusing on language, has been most successful in describing this level of Genet's plays. Genet's characters use language as they use costume, to conceal, to reveal, to deceive, to revolt. The black-white contest towards the end of *The Blacks* is a verbal contest, and "victory" appears to consist in reassigning connotations to words:

FELICITY: Whatever is gentle and kind and good and tender will be black. Milk will be
    black, sugar, rice, the sky, doves, hope, will be black. So will the opera to which we shall
    go, blacks that we are, in black Rolls Royces to hail black kings, to hear brass bands
    beneath chandeliers of black crystal.

(p. 106)

However, it is not *complete* resemanticization that occurs here, but once again a simultaneous entertaining of *two* semantic fields, which renders both equally contingent and artificial. In language as in every other sign system, it is the *gulf* between signifier and signified that Genet creates on stage. A famous—and commonly misinterpreted—example of this technique occurs in *The Screens,* when Leila addresses a glass. The object in question makes the example doubly exemplary, for the eternal brittleness of glass, as well as its transparence, makes it the perfect emblem for Genet's interest in those boundaries most threatened by rupture, those spaces most vulnerable to invasion. Leila, having almost dropped the glass, addresses it: "Stop being an ass or I'll break you!... Break you, you hear me... break you. And then what'll you be? Bits of glass... and bits of broken glass... or fragments... pieces of glass... rubbish. Or else, if I'm nice, shards... splinters!" (p. 61).

Leila's words are part of a theatrical image of which the visible, unbroken glass is the other part. Together they establish an opposition (unbroken-broken / real-potential), one half of which contains a further opposition, engendered by language alone. This second opposition, between two future or potential states of the glass (as "rubbish" and as "sparkling splinters"), is formed by words, or, more precisely, by the connotative differences in words of similar denotation. However, it is only by ignoring the first opposition ((real) unbroken glass vs. (verbal) broken glass) that one can say, as one critic does, that in this little scene Genet "affirms the power of semantics." Taken in its theatrical context, Leila's wordplay *exposes* the power of semantics, and power exposed is (at least momentarily) power *denied,* not affirmed. Thus when Leila acknowledges the Mother's compliment of her verbal game, saying "In my division, I'm unbeatable" (p. 61), the power she claims is implicitly restricted to a small area ("my division"). To mistake verbal power for real power is to fall into the trap of "congealed" signifiers, as did the revolutionaries in *The Balcony* and as do Sir Harold's gang in this play:

> MR. BLANKENSEE: We're the lords of language.
> SIR HAROLD: And to tamper with language is sacrilegious.
>
> (p. 74)

Tampering with language *appears* sacrilegious only to those who have failed to realize that language *is,* precisely, a mode of tampering. In Genet's semiotically aware vision, it is the refusal to tamper with language, the attempt to freeze language, that is, if not sacrilegious, "monumentally stupid."[37] Thus it is Leila who is unbeatable in division (= tampering with and through language), while the colonials have lost the ability to use even those verbal labels which support their power:

> SIR HAROLD: And besides, even if we wanted to, how could we make the *subtle distinction* between an Arab who's a thief and an Arab who's not. How do they themselves manage it? If a Frenchman robs me, that Frenchman's a thief, but if an Arab robs me, he hasn't changed. He's an Arab who's robbed me, and nothing more.
>
> (p. 75)

The boundary that divides the colonials from the Arabs is that of signification, the ability to signify new things with old signs. This ability, as many critics have noted, is shared by Genet himself: "Genet understands words; he writes with ecstasy and simplicity; he understands the tensions of the French language; he loves its paradoxes."[38] This is true, but it is a truth that can lead to the error of equating Genet's sophisticated "understanding" of language (what I have called his semiotic awareness) with an ultimate, positive "love" of language. This equation, which represents yet another nostalgic desire to find some stable affirmation in one otherwise felt to be so "self-contradictory,"[39] so destructive, has the effect, as do all such nostalgic moves, of neutralizing Genet's denial, making it merely a step towards a higher affirmation which is the playwright's "real" achievement or message. What makes this reasoning particularly insidious is that it necessarily devalues Genet's theatrical achievements, rendering his, once again, an "impossible" theater whose impossibility can be excused as it is the vehicle for a poetic triumph: "But his plays are successful not through their form, which is gauche, their symbolism, which is clumsy, their psychology, which is crude, but uniquely because he is a poet with an outstanding gift for words, and a rich ability to create, and celebrate in words a sensual and dominantly visual world."[40] The "visual world" appreciated here is what I have called the "diegetic space" of the plays, the space created by the dialogue. This space exists, at all times in Genet's plays, in tense relation to mimetic space and is frequently undermined by it. To ignore this relationship and this process is to "novelize" Genet's drama, to exile it, in fact, from the very realm—the theatrical—which it exists to occupy.

The charge of "impossibility"—or, rather, the problematic surrounding such a charge—was the point of departure for this study. Concrete denial—the paradox shared in some degree by all avant-garde drama—appears to be doomed to one of two undesirable effects. On the one hand, its experimentation with, or denial of, realistic theater can become so familiar and formulaic as to become a "tradition" in itself: a new mainstream, coopted by the very audience and society it had aimed to disturb. This is the effect Barthes refers to in his comment on *The Balcony,* and it is certainly an effect clearly seen in the countless thematic readings of the play which draw a discursive message out of it, and, in so doing, implicitly identify it with the thesis plays of realism. On the other hand, dramatic recoding can be so extreme as to break its connection with its audience altogether, resulting in performances which make sense only to a small select group of clued-in spectators—theater people themselves—and which are meaningless to the general audience: a *"dialogue des sourds."*[41]

I have tried to show in this study how Genet's drama escapes these two kinds of failure. It does so by a method, or stance, that is *genuinely* dialectical, one that entertains oppositions *without* privileging one of their terms. This method is one of remarkable ideological *restraint,* for it does not, as is usual with dialectical reasoning, oppose thesis to antithesis in order to arrive at a (predetermined) synthesis. Genet's drama, contrary to most interpretations, does not *go anywhere.* Instead it creates and maintains a static dynamic, a paradox reflected in its simultaneous affirmation and denial of all signs. In Genet's plays, signs—actors, characters, costume, spaces, sets—always become not-themselves without thereby ceasing to be what they appear to be:

themselves. Like his *Blacks*, who are both "blacks" and "constructed blacks" (i.e., not blacks), his plays create a world which is always itself and not-itself, a world under erasure.

This dramaturgy, the dramaturgy of yes-and-no, presence and absence, has been Genet's ideal from the very beginning. In a letter to Jean-Jacques Pauvert written after the production, in 1947, of his first play, *The Maids,* Genet speaks of his hope of "obtaining the abolition of characters . . . to the advantage of *signs as distanced as possible from what they should first signify,* but reattaching themselves to this [first signification] in order to unite, by this sole link, the author and the spectator" (my emphasis). [42] Genet did not feel he had accomplished this kind of "communication through ruptured signification" in *The Maids.* In the next three plays, however, his method of doing so—"bringing the stage on the stage" [43]—is actually, and not just metaphorically, realized, with the desired results. Now his characters are "no more on the stage than metaphors [i.e., *signs*] for that which they were to represent" [44]—not characters at all anymore, but actor-character composites, their duality exposed. They are, like all signs, two parts striving to be a whole but, unlike most signs, it is their partitive as much as—or even more than— their unitary nature that emerges here. They are signs which signify, above all, that they are signs.

The uniqueness of Genet's theater lies in its vast capacity for paradox. Of all the modern playwrights committed to deconstructing the traditional code of their medium, it is Genet who succeeds in both deconstructing *and* accomplishing that code, achieving a theater that is neither classical, nor absurdist, but both. The key to this success is the point at which Genet focuses: neither on the past nor the future but on the gap of signification—the void of difference—between them: "Poetry is the rupture (or rather the encounter at the point of rupture) of the visible and the invisible." [45]

Notes

Chapter 1

1. Recent trends in Genet criticism are well represented by the articles in *Obliques* 2 (1972).

2. Richard Coe, *The Vision of Jean Genet* (New York: Grove Press, 1968), 4.

3. "Seulement chez Genet, toute nouvelle expérience, qu'elle soit de l'ordre du vécu ou de la technique littéraire, s'enracine bientôt et profondément dans son univers personnel. Rapidement il la fait sienne. Ainsi, lorsque, par deux fois, il lui arriva d'écrire une pièce sur commande, *Les Bonnes* pour Jouvet, *Les Nègres* pour une compagnie de comédiens noirs, Les Griots, il ne peut le faire qu'en injectant dans le drame ses propres phantasmes." Claude Bonnefoy, *Jean Genet*, Classiques du XXᵉ siècle (Paris: Editions universitaires, 1965), 106 (my translation).

4. "Genet copiait un héros idéal auquel un acteur du milieu, Stilitano ou quelque autre mac, prêtait vie. Pour être Stilitano—belle apparence, collection de gestes déjà empruntés— Genet s'exerçait a lui voler ses gestes." Jean-Marie Magnan, *Essai sur Jean Genet*, Poètes d'aujourd'hui, No. 148 (Paris: Seghers, 1966), 166. (This, and all further quotations from this text, are in my translation.)

5. Ibid. "Et il se peut que *Le Balcon* ait pour principal objet de délivrer Genet des gestes, de le désenchanter."

6. Ibid. "... il se trouve au centre avec Mme Irma et réussit à organiser autour de sa personne ce théâtre fastueux: une fête dont les splendeurs l'enveloppent et le dissimulent au monde."

7. Ibid., 180.

8. Joseph McMahon, *The Imagination of Jean Genet* (New Haven, Conn.: Yale University Press, 1963), 247.

9. Robert Brustein, "Antonin Artaud and Jean Genet: The Theatre of Cruelty," in *The Theatre of Revolt* (Boston, Mass.: Little, Brown, 1964), 361–411.

10. Philip Thody, *Jean Genet: A Study of His Novels and Plays* (New York: Stein and Day, 1969); Lucien Goldmann, "The Theater of Genet: A Sociological Study," *Genet: A Collection of Critical Essays,* ed. Peter Brooks and Joseph Halpern (Englewood Cliffs, N.J.: Prentice-Hall, 1979), 31–46; Lewis Cetta, *Profane Play, Ritual, and Jean Genet* (University, Ala.: University of Alabama Press, 1974).

11. Genet, "A Note on Theatre," trans. Bernard Frechtman, *Tulane Drama Review* 7, no. 3 (Spring 1963): 38.

12. Georges Bataille, "Genet: The Refusal to Communicate," trans. Alastair Hamilton, in *Genet: A Collection of Critical Essays*, ed. Peter Brooks and Joseph Halpern (Englewood Cliffs, N.J.: Prentice-Hall, 1979), 24.

13. Ibid.

14. Ibid., 27.

15. Lionel Abel's *Metatheatre: A New View of Dramatic Form* (New York: Hill and Wang, 1963) gave focus to a wide-ranging thematic critical tradition dedicated to studying the theme of theater in both classical and modern drama. Some representative studies of this critical tradition that focus on modern drama are David Grossvogel's *The Self-Conscious Stage in Modern French Drama* (New York: Columbia University Press, 1958) and June Schlueter's *Metafictional Characters in Modern Drama* (New York: Columbia University Press, 1979). Of the noncritical studies that this tradition frequently makes use of, the major ones are Elizabeth Burns's *Theatricality: A Study of Convention in the Theatre and in Social Life* (London: Longman Group, 1972), Erving Goffman's *The Presentation of Self in Everyday Life* (Garden City, N.Y.: Doubleday, 1959), and Johan Huizinga's *Homo Ludens: A Study of the Play-Element in Culture* (Boston, Mass.: Beacon Press, 1950).

16. Edith Melcher, "The Pirandellism of Jean Genet," *French Review* 36 (October 1962): 36.

17. Stanley Eskin, "Theatricality in the Avant-Garde Drama: A Reconsideration of a Theme in the Light of *The Balcony* and *The Connection*," *Modern Drama*, 7 (1964): 218.

18. Lionel Abel, "*Le Balcon*: Metatheater," *Partisan Review* 27, no. 2 (1960): 329.

19. Patrice Pavis, "The Interplay between Avant-Garde Theatre and Semiology," *Performing Arts Journal* 15, V, no. 3 (1981): 78.
    The "research" aspect of twentieth-century drama has been most widely recognized in the plays of Bertolt Brecht, which are as concerned with conveying meaning as they are with foregrounding the methods and mechanisms by which meanings are constructed and conveyed.

20. "... un auxiliare indispensable dans la recherche de l'apparence." Y. Went-Daoust, "Objets et lieux dans *Le Balcon* de Jean Genet," *Neophilologus* 63 (1979): 23. (This, and all further quotations from this text, are in my translation.)

21. Ibid., 27. "une fixité définitive, fixité idéale de la mort."

22. Ibid., 30. "Les Photographes forment un groupe privilégié par leur profession même. De plain-pied avec le miroir, ils rivalisent avec lui dans l'effort vers la réalisation de l'image."

23. F. Clabecq and J. Blairon, "*Le Balcon*: Autour de quelques objets," *Obliques* 2 (1972): 23.

24. Ibid. "L'importance du texte étant très grande chez Genet, il semble logique d'accorder autant d'importance à une catégorie qu'à une autre et de considérer que toutes trois sont constitutives d'un même univers représenté" (my translation).

25. Michèle Piemme, "Scenic Space and Dramatic Illusion in *The Balcony*," trans. Kathryn Kinczewski, in Brooks and Halpern, eds., 156–71.

26. Ibid., 171.

27. Jean Gitenet, "Profane and Sacred Reality in Jean Genet's Theatre," trans. Janie Vanpée, in Brooks and Halpern, eds., 172–77.

28. Ibid., 174.

Chapter 2

1. Julia Kristeva, *Sémiotikè: Recherches pour une sémanalyse* (Paris: Seuil, 1968), 30–31.

2. See, for example, Anne Ubersfeld's "The Space of Phèdre," *Poetics Today* 2, no. 3 (Spring 1981): 201–10.

3. Representative examples of this stage are to be found in *Semiotics of Art,* ed. Ladislaw Matejka and Irwin R. Titunik (Cambridge, Mass.: MIT Press, 1976).

4. Umberto Eco, "Semiotics of Theatrical Performance," *The Drama Review* 21 (1977): 107–17.

5. Ibid, 109.

6. "[The] notion that the production of new interpretations is the task of literary study, the *raison d'être* of all writing about literature, is now such a fundamental assumption of Anglo-American criticism that it has a decisive impact on all developments in contemporary criticism." Jonathan Culler, *The Pursuit of Signs* (Ithaca, N.Y.: Cornell University Press, 1981), ix.

7. Jonathan Culler, *Structuralist Poetics* (Ithaca, N.Y.: Cornell University Press, 1975), 244.

8. Culler, *Pursuit,* 4.

9. Ibid., 3.

10. Semioticians have tended to use the terms "system" (of signs) and "code" more or less synonymously; recently, an attempt has been made to distinguish them, notably by Umberto Eco, who uses "system" to refer to any repertory of signs or signals along with the internal syntactic rules governing their selection and combination, and "code" to refer to a set of rules that allows correlations between two or more separate systems. See Umberto Eco, *A Theory of Semiotics* (Bloomington, Ind.: Indiana University Press, 1976), 36–37; Keir Elam, *The Semiotics of Theatre and Drama* (London: Methuen, 1980), 49–50.

11. The play, that is, the play *as performed,* gives rise to a set of theatrical *messages*: units of perceived meaning created by the transmission of signs which are chosen and deployed according to certain rules (the *codes*) familiar to both senders and receivers.

12. E.g., Susan Horton, *Interpreting Interpreting: Interpreting Dickens' Dombey* (Baltimore: Johns Hopkins University Press, 1979). Several other ways of undertaking this kind of project are discussed in Culler, "Semiotics as a Theory of Reading," *Pursuit,* 47–49.

13. Tadeusz Kowzan, "The Sign in the Theatre," *Diogenes,* 61 (1968): 52–80. Kowzan identifies thirteen systems, but acknowledges the arbitrariness of this selection, saying "a much more detailed classification could also be made," 61.

14. Elam, *Semiotics,* 51.

15. Ibid., 38.

16. Georges Mounin, *Introduction à la sémiologie* (Paris: Les Editions de Minuit, 1969).

17. Franco Ruffini, "Semiotica del teatro: ricognizione degli studi," *Biblioteca teatrale* 9 (1974): 34–81. Trans. Elam, *Semiotics,* 34.

18. Roman Jakobson, "Linguistics and Poetics," in *Style and Language,* ed. Thomas Sebeok (Cambridge, Mass.: MIT Press, 1960), 353.

19. Culler, *Poetics*, 241.

20. "Les codes théâtraux sont des codes 'ouverts', en perpetuelle évolution." Patrice Pavis, *Dictionnaire du théâtre* (Paris: Editions sociales, 1980), 63 (my translation).

21. Roland Barthes, *Image-Music-Text*, trans. Stephen Heath (New York: Hill and Wang, 1977), 17.

22. Exceptions abound: many social situations are structured in ways that assign special significance to certain otherwise ordinary locations or objects. At a job interview, the interviewee's chair is primarily a sign of his role—a "hot seat"—and only secondarily a simple chair.

23. Keir Elam, "Language in the Theater," *Sub-stance*, No. 18/19 (1977): 144.

24. For example, in simple communications ("You can get the A-Train here"), the speaker's accent, age, appearance can often be completely disregarded; all that matters is that he/she follow the linguistic rules necessary to construct the required sentence.

25. Kowzan, "The Sign," 60.

26. Elam, "Language," 141.

27. It should be noted that the theater is by no means the only "polysystem." Language too is a composite system, comprising a "complex of codes ranging from denotational correlational rules to dialectical, paralinguistic, rhetorical, pragmatic, and contextual rules, all of which go to make up the rich network of constraints regulating utterances and their meanings" (Elam, *Semiotics*, 50).

28. The famous story about Groucho Marx's response to "the scratches on Julie Harris's legs" (quoted in Elizabeth Burns, *Theatricality* [London: Longham, 1972], 36), though often read as an example of the semiotization principle (e.g., Elam, *Semiotics*, 9), is also an example of the variability of sign-perception within an audience.

29. To make my discussion of theatrical signifiers and signifieds easier to follow, I have employed the following graphic convention: words referring to signifiers are enclosed in single slashes (/signifier/), words referring to signifieds in double slashes (//signified//), and words referring to referents—i.e., to actual objects—are enclosed in guillemets («referent»).

30. Jindrich Honzl, "Dynamics of the Sign in the Theater," in Matejka and Titunik, eds., 76.

31. Ibid., 82. "An actor-prop originated by placing next to the actor playing the role of the costume, another actor dressed in blue coveralls who held up the handle of the ship's horn the moment when the captain, pulling the handle, blasts a signal to the sailor." A more famous example is the actor-wall in the comic play-within-the-play of *A Midsummer Night's Dream*.

32. Ibid. "Two 'invisibly' attired actors kneel opposite each other and stretch between them a tablecloth into the quadrilateral shape of a table."

33. Ibid. "in a presentation by Oxlopkov, a metaphor of a storm was shown by an invasion of carnival merrimakers. Boys and girls (actors in blue coveralls) threw confetti at each other while jumping about and generally making noise."

34. Ibid. "Oxlopkov created an actor-sea by having a young man dressed in a neutral manner...shake a blue-green sheet attached to the floor in such a way that the rippling of the blue-green sheet expressively replaced the waves of the sea canal."

35. Ibid. The "invisible" men of the Chinese theater "(dressed in black), who assist in changing scenes, for instance, by covering the bodies of the dead warriors with a black cloth."

36. Ibid., 84.

37. Elam, *Semiotics*, 12. Only the last of these terms seems to me to be inappropriate, for it implies that the theatrical sign moves between different *codes*, whereas in fact it moves only between different systems.

38. Eco, *A Theory*, 217.

39. Elam, *Semiotics*, 12.

40. Eco, *A Theory*, 270.

41. Ibid., 268–70. .

42. Ibid., 274.

43. Ibid., 271.

44. Ibid., 272.

45. Elam, *Semiotics*, 22.

46. Charles Sanders Peirce, *Collected Papers* (Cambridge: Harvard University Press, 1931–58).

47. Charles Morris, *Signs, Language, Behavior* (New York: Prentice-Hall, 1946). Quoted in Eco, *A Theory*, 192.

48. Ibid., 193.

49. Ibid., 180.

50. Ibid.

51. Ferdinand de Saussure, *Course in General Linguistics*, trans. Wade Baskin (New York: McGraw-Hill, 1966), 7–15.

52. Elam, *Semiotics*, 87.

53. Erving Goffman, *Frame Analysis* (Cambridge: Harvard University Press, 1974), 9.

54. Ibid., 10–11.

55. "Pour éviter l'impasse des discussions sur l'essence du théâtre, il faut sans doute se convaincre du fait que l'objet dont il est question n'est pas donné: il ne peut être qu'un objet *construit* par l'analyste." Régis Durand, "Problèmes de l'analyse structurale et sémiotique de la forme théâtrale," in *Sémiologie de la représentation*, ed. André Helbo (Brussels: Complexe, 1975), 112.

56. Antonin Artaud, *The Theater and Its Double*, trans. Mary Caroline Richards (New York: Grove Press, 1958), 74–83.

57. "Jean Genet in a Temper," in *The Theater of Jean Genet: A Casebook*, ed. Richard Coe (New York: Grove Press, 1970), 88.

58. Jean Genet, "I have been the victim of an attempted murder!" in Coe, *Casebook*, 90.

59. Roland Barthes, *Critical Essays*, trans. Richard Howard (Evanston: Northwestern University Press, 1972), 74.

60. E.g., Jean Genet, *Letters to Roger Blin*, trans. Richard Seaver (New York: Grove Press, 1969).

Chapter 3

1. The term postmodern, like the term avant-garde, has been used very differently in different contexts. Both terms are used to describe works belonging to certain historical periods (again, without general agreement or consensus) as well as to describe certain *qualities* of works. In this study, I employ the first usage for the term avant-garde (to designate post-Realist experiments dating from Alfred Jarry) and the second usage for the term postmodern (to designate a certain dramatic method distinguished by its subversive or deconstructive relationship to previous dramatic codes).

2. Barthes, "*Le Balcon*. Mise en scène de Peter Brook au Théâtre du Gymnase," *Obliques* 2 (1972): 38. "Genet subit aujourd'hui le sort de tout théâtre avant-garde, immanquablement liquidé, du jour òu il est reconnu par le public avec lequel il prétend rompre. . . . On peut dire que *Le Balcon* accomplit une loi inflexible: il était fatale que Genet fut un jour acclimaté: ce jour est venu" (my translation).

3. Jacques Derrida, *Glas* (Paris: Editions Galilée, 1975).

4. Jacques Derrida, *Of Grammatology*, trans. Gayatri C. Spivak (Baltimore, Md.: Johns Hopkins University Press, 1974).

5. Spivak, "Translator's Preface," ibid., xv.

6. Ibid.

7. See, for example, *Semiotext(e): Nietzsche's Return* 3, no. 1 (1978).

8. *On the Genealogy of Morals, and Ecce Homo*, trans. Walter Kaufman (New York: Vintage Books, 1969), 238.

9. Spivak, xxviii.

10. Derrida, *Grammatology*, 18.

11. Spivak, xvi.

12. Ibid., xxix.

13. Jean Genet, *Letters*, 47.

14. In light of the problematic involved in iconicity (outlined in chapter 2), the concept of the iconic sign is necessarily vague. I use it here simply to designate those signs which, at least at the first stage of perception, resemble, more or less closely, the real-world objects they stand for. Genet's use of such signs, we shall see, always puts their alleged iconicity into question by foregrounding the difference between their real-world and their theatrical functions. The costumes, the mirrors, the actors, are all instances of such pseudoiconic signs.

15. Jean Genet, *The Balcony*, rev. ed., trans. Bernard Frechtman (New York: Grove Press, 1966), 7. All further page references to this text will appear in parentheses after the quotations.

16. Eco, *A Theory*, 266.

17. Ibid.

18. Peter and Linda Murray, *A Dictionary of Art and Artists* (Harmondsworth: Penguin, 1959), 319.

19. William M. Ivins, Jr., *On the Rationalization of Sight* (New York: Da Capo Press, 1975). Quoted in Richard Palmer, "Toward a Postmodern Hermeneutics of Performance," *Performance in Postmodern Culture,* ed. M. Benamou and C. Caramello (Madison, Wis.: Coda Press, 1977), 21.

20. Ibid.

21. Ibid., 21, 22.

22. Ibid., 22–23.

23. Genet, "A Note," 38.

24. Jean Genet, "Comment jouer *Le Balcon*," *Le Balcon* (Version definitive, 9 scènes) (Decines: L'Arbalète, 1961), 10.

25. Eco, *A Theory,* 202.

26. Julia Kristeva, "Modern Theater Does Not Take (a) Place," *Sub-stance* 18/19 (1977): 131–34.

27. Victor Turner, "Frame, Flow and Reflection: Ritual and Drama as Public Liminality," in Benamou and Caramello, eds., 35.

28. Perhaps I should say "will not" or "must not" be prevented, for, as I will show later, the invasion of privacy is not a *fault* but a necessity of the theatrical system.

29. One is reminded, significantly, of the "Panopticon" described by Michel Foucault in his study of prisons: *Discipline and Punish: The Birth of the Prison,* trans. Alan Sheridan (New York: Pantheon Books, 1977).

30. Eco, *A Theory,* 7.

31. Ibid., 202.

32. A recent article by Dina Sherzer ("Frames and Metacommunications in Genet's *The Balcony,*" in *Semiotics of Drama and Theatre,* ed. Herta Schmid and Aloysius Van Kesteren [Amsterdam and Philadelphia: John Benjamins Publishing Company, 1984], 368–392) contains approaches and insights similar to those in this chapter. Unfortunately, Sherzer's article appeared too late in the preparation of this book to allow me to incorporate a proper discussion of it here.

Chapter 4

1. Jean Genet *The Blacks: A Clown Show,* trans. Bernard Frechtman (New York: Grove Press, 1960), 84. All further page references to this text will appear in parentheses after the quotations.

2. The distinction between mimesis (representation; direct imitation) and diegesis (narration; description) corresponds to the distinction between "showing" and "telling" made by narratologists. E.g., Wayne C. Booth, *The Rhetoric of Fiction* (Chicago: University of Chicago Press, 1961), 3–20.

3. William James, *Principles of Psychology,* Vol. 2 (New York: Dover Publications, 1950), 291.

4. Goffman, *Frame Analysis,* 2.

5. Elam, *Semiotics,* 104.

6. E.g., Elam, "Language," 145.

7. J. L. Austin, *How to Do Things with Words* (London: Oxford University Press, 1962), 21–22.

8. E.g., Richard Ohmann, "Literature as Act," in *Approaches to Poetics,* ed. Seymour Chatman (New York: Columbia University Press, 1973), 81–107.

9. Elam, *Semiotics,* 99–100.

10. For example, Richard Coe concludes his discussion of the play by saying: "The Blacks are shown entirely without fear. They have already won.... Such fear as there is (mainly concealed), is on the side of the whites" (*Vision,* 296). This conclusion, like the analysis that preceded it, ignores the fact that there are *no whites* in the play.

11. Goffman cites *The Blacks* as an example of what he calls "the theater of frames"—the "so-called theater of the absurd" (399).

12. Ibid., 125.

13. Elam, "Language," 144.

14. Gregory Bateson, "A Theory of Play and Fantasy," in *Steps to an Ecology of Mind* (London: Granada Publishing, 1973), 150–66.

15. Ibid., 151.

16. Ibid.

17. Ibid., 152.

18. Ibid., 153.

19. Ibid.

20. Eco, "Semiotics," 108.

21. Ibid., 117.

22. Susan Sontag, *Styles of Radical Will* (New York: Dell, 1970), 169–70.

23. See, for example, William Sacksteder, "Elements of the Dramatic Model," *Diogenes* 52 (1975): 26–54.

24. Bateson, 154.

25. Jean-Paul Sartre, "Introduction," to Jean Genet, *The Maids and Deathwatch,* trans. Bernard Frechtman (New York: Grove Press, 1954), 8–9.

26. Goffman, 129.

27. Elam, *Semiotics,* 110.

28. Goffman, 130.

29. Ibid., 126.

30. Ibid., 130.

31. "THE GOVERNOR: Be quiet, you whippersnapper! You and your damned exoticism!" (p. 19).

32. Quoted in Elam, *Semiotics,* 10.

33. THE VALET (*looking about him*): What's happened to my chair?
    THE MISSIONARY (*doing the same*): And to mine? Who took it?

    (p. 11)

34. Elam, *Semiotics,* 112.

35. Goffman, 269.

36. Ibid., 270.

37. Ibid., 275.

38. Ibid., 274.

39. Ibid., 133.

40. Ibid., 149–50.

41. Ibid., 47.

Chapter 5

1. Roland Barthes, "Racine Is Racine," *The Eiffel Tower and Other Mythologies,* trans. Richard Howard (New York: Hill and Wang, 1979), 59.

2. Coe, *Vision,* 308–9.

3. Ibid.

4. Barthes, "Racine," 61.

5. Bernard Dort, "Genet: The Struggle with Theater," in Brooks and Halpern, 115.

6. Ibid., 117.

7. Lucien Goldmann,"The Theater of Jean Genet: A Sociological Study," in Brooks and Halpern, 31.

8. Ibid., 42–43.

9. Ibid., 39.

10. Jean Genet, *Letters,* 67.

11. Goldmann, 41.

12. Quoted in Dort, 120.

13. Goldmann, 43.

14. Ibid., 32.

15. Lucien Goldmann, "Une pièce réaliste: *Le Balcon* de Genet," *Les Temps modernes* 15, no. 171 (June 1960). Quoted in Dort, 117.

16. Ibid.

17. Dort, 117.

18. Genet, "Comment jouer *Les Bonnes,*" *Les Bonnes* (Paris: L'Arbalète, 1963), p. 11.

19. Quoted in Dort, 116.

20. Genet, "Comment jouer *Le Balcon,*" 10.

21. Dort, 119.

22. Ibid., 124.

23. Coe, *Vision*, 309.

24. Jean Genet, "Lettre à Pauvert sur *Les Bonnes*" (Sceaux: J. J. Pauvert, 1954), 147.

25. Thody, 205.

26. Michael Issacharoff, "Space and Reference in Drama," *Poetics Today* 2, no. 3 (Spring 1981), 211–24.

27. Elam, *Semiotics*.

28. Jean Genet, *The Screens*, trans. Bernard Frechtman (New York: Grove Press, 1962), 145. All further page references to this text will appear in parentheses after the quotations.

29. Henrik Ibsen, *Ghosts*, trans. Rolf Fjelde (New York: New American Library, 1970), 70.

30. Shoshana Avigal and Shlomith Rimmon-Kenan, "What Do Brook's Bricks Mean? Toward a Theory of the 'Mobility' of Objects in Theatrical Discourse," *Poetics Today* 2, no. 3 (Spring 1981): 11.

31. Petr Bogatyrev, "Les Signes du théâtre," *Poétiques* 8 (1971): 517.

32. Avigal and Rimmon-Kenan, 18.

33. Ibid., 22.

34. Ibid.

35. Ibid., 22–23.

36. Anne Ubersfeld, *Lire le théâtre* (Paris: Editions sociales, 1977), 40–44, 248–72.

37. Jean Genet, *Letters*, 66. "The soldier scenes are meant to exalt—and I mean *exalt*—the Army's prime, its chief, virtue: stupidity."

38. Gary O'Connor, *French Theatre Today* (London: Pitman Publishing Company, 1975), 58.

39. Ibid.

40. Ibid.

41. Avigal and Rimmon-Kennan, 23.

42. "J'espérais obtenir ainsi l'abolition des personnages—qui ne tiennent d'habitude que par convention psychologique—au profit de signes aussi éloignés que possible de ce qu'ils doivent d'abord signifier, mais s'y rattachant tout de même afin d'unir par ce seul lien l'auteur au spectateur." Jean Genet, "A Pauvert," *Obliques* 2: 3. (This, and all further quotations from this text, are in my translation.)

43. Ibid. "porterait le théâtre sur le théâtre."

44. Ibid. "que ces personnages ne fussent plus sur la scène que la métaphore de ce qu'ils devaient représenter."

45. "La poésie est la rupture (ou plutôt la rencontre au point de rupture) du visible et de l'invisible." Jean Genet, *Obliques* 2: 64.

Selected Bibliography

Works by Jean Genet

"L'Atelier d'Alberto Giacometti." *Lettres nouvelles* (September 1957).
Le Balcon, preceded by *Comment jouer Le Balcon*. Paris: L'Arbalète, 1962.
The Balcony. Trans. Bernard Frechtman. New York: Grove Press, 1958.
The Blacks, A Clown Show. Trans. Bernard Frechtman. New York: Grove Press, 1960.
Les Bonnes, preceded by *Comment jouer Les Bonnes*. Paris: L'Arbalète, 1963.
"A candid conversation with the brazen brilliant author of *The Balcony* and *The Blacks*, self-proclaimed homosexual, coward, thief and traitor." *Playboy* (April 1964).
The Funambulist. Trans. Bernard Frechtman. *Evergreen Review* 32 (April-May 1966).
Haute Surveillance. Paris: Gallimard, 1965.
"Letter from Paris," *New Yorker* 29, no. 44 (December 1953).
Letters to Roger Blin. Trans. Richard Seaver. New York: Grove Press, 1969.
Lettre à J.-J. Pauvert sur Les Bonnes. Sceaux: J.-J. Pauvert, 1954.
The Maids and Death Watch. Trans. Bernard Frechtman. New York: Grove Press, 1954.
Les Nègres, preceded by *Comment jouer Les Nègres*. Paris: L'Arbalète, 1960.
"A Note on Theater." Trans. Bernard Frechtman. *Tulane Drama Review* (Spring 1963): 37-41.
Les Paravents. Paris: L'Arbalète, 1961.
The Screens. Trans. Bernard Frechtman. New York: Grove Press, 1962.
"To a Would-Be Producer." Trans. Bernard Frechtman. *Tulane Drama Review* (Spring 1963): 80-81.

Works on Jean Genet

Books (Including Collections of Essays)

Bonnefoy, Claude. *Jean Genet*. Classiques du XXe siècle. Paris: Editions universitaires, 1965.
Brooks, Peter, and Joseph Halpern, eds. *Genet: A Collection of Critical Essays*. Englewood Cliffs, N.J.: Prentice-Hall, 1979.
Cetta, Lewis T. *Profane Play, Ritual, and Jean Genet*. University, Ala.: University of Alabama Press, 1974.
Choukri, Mohamed. *Jean Genet in Tangier*. Trans. Paul Bowles. New York: Ecco Press, 1974.
Coe, Richard N., ed. *The Theater of Jean Genet: A Casebook*. New York: Grove Press, 1970.
_____. *The Vision of Jean Genet*. New York: Grove Press, 1968.
Driver, Tom F. *Jean Genet*. Columbia Essays on Modern Writers No. 20. New York: Columbia University Press, 1966.

Henning, Sylvie D. *Genet's Ritual Play.* Amsterdam: Rodopi, 1981.

Knapp, Bettina. *Jean Genet.* Twayne World Authors Series No. 44. New York: Twayne, 1968.

Magnan, Jean-Marie. *Essai sur Jean Genet.* Poètes d'aujourd'hui. Paris: Seghers, 1966.

McMahon, Joseph H. *The Imagination of Jean Genet.* New Haven: Yale University Press, 1963.

Morris, Kelley, ed. *Genet/Ionesco: The Theater of the Double.* New York: Bantam Books, 1969.

Naish, Camille. *A Genetic Approach to Structures in the Works of Jean Genet.* Cambridge, Mass.: Harvard University Press, 1978.

Obliques 2 (1972). Special issue on Genet.

Sartre, Jean-Paul. *Saint Genet: Actor and Martyr.* Trans. Bernard Frechtman. New York: George Braziller, 1963.

Savona, Jeanette Laillou. *Jean Genet.* New York: Grove Press, 1984.

Thody, Philip. *Jean Genet: A Study of His Novels and Plays.* London: Hamish Hamilton; New York: Stein and Day, 1969.

Tulane Drama Review 7 (Spring 1963). Special issue on Genet and Ionesco.

Webb, Richard C., and Suzanne A. Webb. *Jean Genet and His Critics: An Annotated Bibliography 1943–1980.* Methuen, N.J.: Scarecrow, 1982.

Yale French Studies 29 (Spring/Summer 1962). Special issue devoted to "The New Dramatists."

Articles, Essays, and Books Partially Devoted to Genet

Abel, Lionel. "*Le Balcon:* Metatheater." Partisan Review 27, no. 2, (1960): 324–30.

———. *Metatheatre: A New View of Dramatic Form.* New York: Hill and Wang, 1963, 76–82.

Adler, Thomas P. "The Mirror as Stage Prop in Modern Drama." *Comparative Drama* 14 (1980): 355–73.

Aslan, Odette. "Genet, His Actors and Directors." Trans. Elaine Ancekewicz. In *Genet: A Collection of Critical Essays.* Ed. Peter Brooks and Joseph Halpern, 146–55. Englewood Cliffs, N.J.: Prentice-Hall, 1979.

Barbour, Thomas. "Playwrights or Play-Writers." *Hudson Review* 7 (1954): 470–75.

Barthes, Roland. "*Le Balcon:* Mise en scène de Peter Brook au Théâtre du Gymnase." *Obliques* 2 (1972): 37–38.

Bataille, Georges. *Literature and Evil.* Trans. Alastair Hamilton. London: Calder and Boyars, 1973, 145–79.

Bermel, Albert. "Society as a Brothel: Genet's Satire in *The Balcony.*" *Modern Drama* 19 (1976): 265–80.

Bertman, Martin A. "A Metaphysical Analysis of Genet's *Le Balcon.*" *Agora* 4 (1979–80): 78–84.

Biner, Pierre. *The Living Theater.* New York: Horizon Press, 1972, 102–10.

Birn, Randi Marie. "Claudel's *L'Annonce faite à Marie* and Genet's *Le Balcon:* Similarities in Ritual Theater." *Romance Notes* 13 (1971): 1–7.

Bishop, Thomas. *Pirandello and the French Theater.* New York: New York University Press, 1960, 138–39.

Blau, Herbert. *The Impossible Theater: A Manifesto.* New York: Macmillan, 1964, 261–76.

Borie, Monique. "Genet ou le cérémonial-simulacre et l'irréalisation des mythologies." In *Mythe et théâtre aujourd'hui: Une Quête impossible? Beckett, Genet, Grotowski, le Living Theatre.* Paris: Nizet, 1981, 69–116.

Botsford, Keith. "But He Writes Like an Angel." *New York Times Magazine* (February 27, 1972): 16–17.

———. "Jean Genet." *Yale French Studies,* No. 8 (1951): 82–92.

Brustein, Robert. *The Theatre of Revolt.* Boston: Little, Brown, 1964, 361–411.

Butor, Michel. "*Les Paravents.*" *Obliques* 2, (1962): 54–59.

Calarco, N. Joseph. "Vision without Compromise: Genet's *The Screens,*" *Drama Survey* 4 (Spring 1965): 44–50.

Cetta, Lewis T. "Jean Genet as Guru: A Note on the Ending of *The Screens*." *Notes on Contemporary Literature* 1 (May 1971): 11–13.

———. "Jean Genet as *Homo Ludens* in Quest of Profane Play." *Connecticut Review* 6 (October 1972): 26–33.

———. "Myth, Magic, and Play in Genet's *The Blacks*." *Contemporary Literature* 11 (1970): 511–25.

Chiaromonte, Nicola. "Jean Genet, White and Black." *Partisan Review* 28 (1961): 662–68.

Clabecq, Françoise, and Jean Blairon. "*Le Balcon:* Autour de quelques objets." *Obliques* 2 (1972): 23–31.

Clark, Eleanor. "The World of Jean Genet." *Partisan Review* 16 (1949): 442–48.

Clurman, Harold. *The Divine Pastime*. New York: Macmillan, 1974, 304–8.

———. *The Naked Image*. New York: Macmillan, 1966, 72–76.

Coe, Richard N. "Unbalanced Opinions: Jean Genet and the French Critics." *Proceedings of the Leeds Philosophical and Literary Society* 14 (1970): 27–73.

Cohn, Ruby. "Dialogue of Cruelty." *Southern Review* 3 (1967): 322–40.

———. "*Theatrum Mundi* and Contemporary Theater." *Comparative Drama* 1 (Spring 1967): 28–35.

Corrigan, Robert. "The Theater in Search of a Fix." *Tulane Drama Review* 5 (June 1961): 21–35.

Cruickshank, John. "Jean Genet: The Aesthetics of Crime." *Critical Quarterly* 6 (1964): 202–10.

Curtis, Jerry L. "The World Is a Stage: Sartre versus Genet." *Modern Drama* 17 (1974): 33–41.

Dace, Letitia. "On Jean Genet and Martin Esslin, or Here Absurdist, There Absurdist, Everywhere...." *Kansas Quarterly* 3 (Spring 1971): 110–16.

Deguy, Michel. "Théâtre et réalisme: Le cas des *Paravents*." *Obliques* 2 (1972): 51–55.

Dejean, Jean-Luc. *Le Théâtre français d'aujourd'hui*. Paris: Fernand Nathan, 1971.

Donohue, Walter. "Production Casebook No. 13: Genet's *The Screens*." *Theatre Quarterly* 4 (February-April 1974): 74–91.

———. "Total Immersion." *Gambit* 23 (1963): 61–67.

Dort, Bernard. "Genet et Pirandello ou d'un théâtre de la représentation." *Lendemains* 19 (1980): 73–83.

———. "Genet: The Stuggle with Theater." Trans. Ruth Goldfarb. In *Genet: A Collection of Critical Essays*. Ed. Peter Brooks and Joseph Halpern, 114–28. Englewood Cliffs, N.J.: Prentice-Hall, 1979.

Driver, Tom F. "The Spiritual Diabolism of Jean Genet." *Christian Century* (November 20, 1963): 1433–35.

Ehrmann, Jacques. "Genet's Dramatic Metamorphosis: From Appearance to Freedom." *Yale French Studies* 29 (1962): 33–42.

Eskin, Stanley G. "Theatricality in the Avant-Garde Drama: A Reconsideration of a Theme in the Light of *The Balcony* and *The Connection*." *Modern Drama* 7 (1964): 213–22.

Esslin, Martin. *The Theatre of the Absurd*. Garden City, N.Y.: Doubleday, 1961, 140–97.

Federman, Raymond. "Genet: The Theatre of Hate." Trans. Frank Abetti. In *Genet: A Collection of Critical Essays*. Ed. Peter Brooks and Joseph Halpern, 129–45. Englewood Cliffs, N.J.: Prentice-Hall, 1979.

Fichte, Hubert. "I Allow Myself to Revolt." Interview with Jean Genet. Trans. Christa Dove. In *Genet: A Collection of Critical Essays*. Ed. Peter Brooks and Joseph Halpern, 178–90. Englewood Cliffs, N.J.: Prentice-Hall, 1979.

Fowlie, Wallace. *Dionysus in Paris*. New York: Meridian Books, 1958, 218–22.

———. "The New French Theater: Artaud, Beckett, Genet, Ionesco." *Sewanee Review* 67 (1959): 643–57.

———. "New Plays of Ionesco and Genet." *Tulane Drama Review* 5, no. 1 (September 1960): 43–48.

Francovitch, Allan. "Genet's Theater of Possession." *The Drama Review* 14 (Fall 1969): 25–45.

Gitenet, Jean. "Lecture sémiologique des annotations de décor du tableau 4 du *Balcon.*" *Obliques* 2 (1972): 32–36.

———. "Réalité profane et réalité sacrée dans le théâtre de Jean Genet." *Obliques* 2 (1972): 70–73. Trans. Janie Vanpée as "Profane and Sacred Reality in Jean Genet's Theatre." In *Genet: A Collection of Critical Essays.* Ed. Peter Brooks and Joseph Halpern, 172–77. Englewood Cliffs, N.J.: Prentice-Hall, 1979.

Goldmann, Lucien. "Une pièce réaliste: *Le Balcon* de Genet." *Les Temps modernes* 15, no. 171 (June 1960): 1885–96.

———. "The Theater of Genet: A Sociological Study." In *Genet: A Collection of Critical Essays.* Ed. Peter Brooks and Joseph Halpern, 31–46. Englewood Cliffs, N.J.: Prentice-Hall, 1979.

Grossvogel, David I. "Genet: The Difficulty of Defining." In *Four Playwrights and a Postscript.* Ithaca, N.Y.: Cornell University Press, 1962, 133–74.

Guicharnaud, Jacques. *Modern French Theater from Giraudoux to Beckett.* Rev. ed. New Haven, Conn.: Yale University Press, 1967, 259–76.

Hervic, Elisabeth. "L'Espace des *Paravents*, espace d'un mystère." *Revue d'histoire du théâtre* 35 (1983): 251–66.

Hauptmann, Robert. "Jean Genet: Evil Apotheosized." In *The Pathological Vision: Jean Genet, Louis-Ferdinand Celine, and Tennessee Williams.* Frankfurt: Lang, 1983, 3–50.

Hughes, Catharine. "Jean Genet and His World of Illusion." *The Critic* (August-September 1961): 20–21, 71–72.

Innes, Christopher. *Holy Theatre: Ritual and the Avant-garde.* Cambridge: Cambridge University Press, 1981.

Jacquemont, Christiane V. "The Essence of the Game and Its Locus in Jean Genet's *Le Balcon.*" *French Review* 53 (1980): 282–87.

Killinger, John. "Jean Genet and Scapegoat Drama." *Comparative Literature Studies* 3 (1966): 207–21.

Knapp, Bettina. "An Interview with Roger Blin." *Tulane Drama Review* 7 (1963): 111–26.

Kott, Jan. "The Icon and the Absurd." *The Drama Review* 14 (1969): 17–24.

Kruger, Loren. "Ritual into Myth: Ceremony and Communication in *The Blacks.*" *Critical Arts* 1, no. 3 (1980): 59–69.

Lecuyer, Maurice. "*Les Nègres* et au-delà." *Obliques* 2 (1972): 44–47.

Mailer, Norman. "The Blacks." *The Village Voice* (May 11, 1961): 11, 14; (May 18, 1961): 11, 14–15.

Markus, Thomas B. "Jean Genet: The Theater of the Perverse." *Educational Theatre Journal* 14 (1962): 209–14.

———. "The Psychological Universe of Jean Genet." *Drama Survey* 3 (1964): 386–92.

Marowitz, Charles. "Brook in Perspective: Digression." *Obliques* 2 (1972): 37–38.

———. "Notes on the Theater of Cruelty." *Tulane Drama Review* 11 (Winter 1966): 152–73.

———. "The Revenge of Jean Genet." *Encore* 8 (September 1961): 17–24.

Martin, Graham Dunstan. "Racism in Genet's *Les Nègres.*" *Modern Language Review* 70 (1975): 517–25.

Melançon, Joseph. "Theatre as Semiotic Practice." *Modern Drama* 25 (1982): 17–24.

Melcher, Edith. "The Pirandellism of Jean Genet." *French Review* 36 (1962): 32–36.

Millett, Kate. *Sexual Politics.* Garden City, N.Y.: Doubleday, 1970, 336–61.

Murch, Anne C. "Bordel et (im)puissance mâle: les quatre premiers tableaux du *Balcon* de Jean Genet." *New Zealand Journal of French Studies* 3, i (1982): 42–65.

Nelson, Benjamin. "*The Balcony* and Parisian Existentialism," *Tulane Drama Review* 7 (1963): 60–79.

Nugent, Robert. "Sculpture into Drama: Giacometti's Influence on Genet." *Drama Survey* 3 (1964): 378–85.

O'Connor, Gary. *French Theatre Today.* London: Pitman, 1975.

Piemme, Michèle. "Espace scénique et illusion dramatique dans *Le Balcon*." *Obliques* 2 (1972): 23–31. Trans. Kathryn Kinczewski as "Scenic Space and Dramatic Illusion in *The Balcony*." In *Genet: A Collection of Critical Essays.* Ed. Peter Brooks and Joseph Halpern, 156–71. Englewood Cliffs, N.J.: Prentice-Hall, 1979.

Pierret, Marc. "Genet's New Play: *The Screens: Tulane Drama Review* 7 (1963): 93–97.

Pritchett, V.S. "Black and White Murder Show." *New Statesman* (June 9, 1961): 928.

Pronko, Leonard. *Avant-Garde: The Experimental Theater in France.* Berkeley: University of California Press, 1962, 140–53.

———. "Jean Genet's *Les Paravents*." *L'Esprit créateur* 2 (1962): 181–88.

Pucciani, Oreste F. "Tragedy, Genet and *The Maids*." *Tulane Drama Review* 7 (1963): 42–59.

Reck, Rima D. "Appearance and Reality in Genet's *Le Balcon*." *Yale French Studies* 29 (Spring-Summer 1962): 20–25.

Scarborough, Margaret. "The Radical Idealism of *The Screens*." *Modern Drama* 15 (1961): 355–68.

Schechner, Richard. "Genet's *The Balcony*: A 1981 Perspective on a 1979/80 Production." *Modern Drama* 25 (1982): 82–104.

Schmeling, Manfred. *Metathéâtre et intertexte: aspects du théâtre dans le théâtre.* Paris: Lettres modernes, 1982, 71–79.

Serreau, Geneviève. "Jean Genet." In *Histoire du 'Nouveau Théâtre.'* Paris: Gallimard, 1966, 117–37.

Sherzer, Dina. "Frames and Metacommunication in Genet's *The Balcony*." In *Semiotics of Drama and Theatre.* Ed. Herta Schmid and Aloysius Van Kesteren, 368–392. Amsterdam and Philadelphia: John Benjamins Publishing Company, 1984.

Sohlich, W. F. "Genet's *The Blacks* and *The Screens*: Dialectic of Refusal and Revolutionary Consciousness." *Comparative Drama* 10 (1976): 216–34.

———. "Genet's Drama: Rites of Passage of the Anti-Hero: From Alienated Existence to Artistic Alienation." *Modern Language Notes* 89 (1974): 641–53.

Strem, George C. "The Theater of Jean Genet: Facets of Illusion—The Anti-Christ and the Underdog." *Minnesota Review* 4 (1964): 226–36.

Svendsen, M. M. "Corydon Revisited: A Reminder on Genet." *Tulane Drama Review* 7 (1963): 98–110.

Swander, Homer D. "Shakespeare and the Harlem Clowns: Illusion and Comic Form in Genet's *The Blacks*." *Yale Review* 55 (1965): 209–227.

Taubes, Susan. "The White Mask Falls." *Tulane Drama Review* 7 (1963): 85–92.

Vasseur, Yves. "Les Objets dans *Les Bonnes*." *Obliques* 2 (1972): 11–19.

Wellwarth, George E. "Jean Genet: The Theater of Illusion and Distillation." In *The Theater of Protest and Paradox.* New York: New York University Press, 1964, 113–33.

———. "The New Dramatists: 3, Jean Genet." *Drama Survey* 1, no. 3 (1962): 308–20.

Went-Daoust, Y. "Objets et lieux dans *Le Balcon* de Jean Genet." *Neophilologus* 63 (1979): 23–43.

Wilcocks, Robert. "Genet's Preoccupation with Language." *Modern Language Review* 65 (1970): 785–92.

Yaeger, Henry J. "The Uncompromising Morality of Jean Genet." *French Review* 39 (1965): 214–19.

Zadek, Peter. "Acts of Violence." *The New Statesman* 4 (1957): 568–70.

Zimbardo, R. A. "Genet's Black Mass." *Modern Drama* 8 (1965): 247–58.

Semiotics, Theater, and Drama Theory

Books and Collections of Essays

Artaud, Antonin. *The Theater and Its Double.* Trans. Mary Caroline Richards. New York: Grove Press, 1958.

Austin, John L. *How to Do Things with Words.* London: Oxford University Press, 1962.

Barthes, Roland. *The Eiffel Tower and Other Mythologies.* Trans. Richard Howard. New York: Hill and Wang, 1979.

————. *Elements of Semiology.* Trans. Annette Lavers and Colin Smith. London: Cape, 1967.

————. *Image-Music-Text.* Trans. Stephen Heath. New York: Hill and Wang, 1977.

Beckerman, Bernard. *Dynamics of Drama.* New York: Knopf, 1970.

Benamou, Michel, and Charles Caramello, eds. *Performance in Postmodern Culture.* Madison, Wis.: Coda Press, 1977.

Benjamin, Walter. *Understanding Brecht.* Trans. Anna Bostock. London: N.L.B., 1973.

Bentley, Eric, ed. *The Theory of the Modern Stage.* Harmondsworth: Penguin, 1968.

Birdwhistell, Ray L. *Kinesics and Context: Essays on Body-Motion Communication.* Harmondsworth: Penguin, 1971.

Bouissac, Paul. *Circus and Culture: A Semiotic Approach.* Bloomington: Indiana University Press, 1976.

————. *La Mesure des gestes: Prolégomènes à la sémiotique gesturelle.* The Hague: Mouton, 1973.

Bourgy, V., and Régis Durand. *La Relation théâtrale.* Lille: Presses de l'Université de Lille, 1980.

Brecht, Bertolt. *Brecht on Theater.* Ed. John Willet. London: Eyre Methuen, 1964.

Brook, Peter. *The Empty Space.* Harmondsworth: Penguin, 1968.

Burns, Elizabeth. *Theatricality: A Study of Convention in the Theatre and in Social Life.* London: Longman, 1972.

Burns, Elizabeth, and Tom Burns. *Sociology of Literature and Drama.* Harmondsworth: Penguin, 1973.

Corti, Maria. *An Introduction to Literary Semiotics.* Trans. Margherita Bogat and Allen Mandelbaum. Bloomington: Indiana University Press, 1978.

Culler, Jonathan. *The Pursuit of Signs.* Ithaca: Cornell University Press, 1981.

————. *Structuralist Poetics.* Ithaca, N.Y.: Cornell University Press, 1975.

De Marinis, Marco. *Semiotica del teatro: L'Analisi testuale dello spettacolo.* Milan: Bompiani, 1982.

Derrida, Jacques. *Glas.* Paris: Editions Galilée, 1975.

————. *Of Grammatology.* Trans. Gayatri Chakravorty Spivak. Baltimore: Johns Hopkins University Press, 1974.

————. *Writing and Difference.* Trans. Alan Bass. Chicago: University of Chicago Press, 1978.

Dort, Bernard, and Anne Ubersfeld, eds. *Le Texte et la scène: Etudes sur l'espace et l'acteur.* Paris: Institut d'Etudes Théâtrales, 1978.

Duvignaud, Jean. *L'Acteur: Esquisse d'une sociologie du comédien.* Paris: P.U.F., 1965.

————. *Sociologie du théâtre: Essai sur les ombres collectives.* Paris: P.U.F., 1963.

Eco, Umberto. *The Role of the Reader: Explorations in the Semiotics of Texts.* Bloomington: Indiana University Press, 1979.

————. *A Theory of Semiotics.* Bloomington: Indiana University Press, 1976.

Elam, Keir. *The Semiotics of Theatre and Drama.* London: Methuen, 1980.

Etudes littéraires 13 (1980): 381–571. Special issue on "Théâtre et théâtralité: Essais d'études sémiotiques."

Foreman, Richard. *Plays and Manifestos.* Ed. Kate Davy. New York: New York University Press, 1976.

Frye, Northrop. *Anatomy of Criticism*. Princeton: Princeton University Press, 1957.

Garvin, Paul L., ed. *A Prague School Reader on Esthetics, Literary Structure and Style*. Washington: Georgetown University Press, 1964.

Goffman, Erving. *Encounters*. Harmondsworth: Penguin, 1972.

———. *Frame Analysis*. Cambridge, Mass.: Harvard University Press, 1974.

———. *Interaction Ritual*. Garden City, N.Y.: Doubleday, 1967.

———. *The Presentation of Self in Everyday Life*. Garden City, N.Y.: Doubleday, 1959.

Goldman, Michael. *The Actor's Freedom: Toward a Theory of Drama*. New York: Viking Press, 1975.

Greimas, A.J. *Du sens*. Paris: Seuil, 1970.

Grotowski, Jerzy. *Towards a Poor Theatre*. New York: Simon and Schuster, 1968.

Hall, Edward T. *The Hidden Dimension* Garden City, N.Y.: Doubleday, 1966.

———. *The Silent Language*. Garden City, N.Y.: Doubleday, 1959.

Hawkes, Terence. *Structuralism and Semiotics*. London: Methuen, 1977.

Helbo, André, ed. *Sémiologie de la représentation*. Brussels: Complexe, 1975.

Hess-Luttich, Ernest, ed. *Multimedial Communication. Vol. I: Theatre Semiotics*, Tubingen: Narr, 1981.

Hornby, Richard. *Script into Performance: A Structuralist View of Play Production*. Austin: University of Texas Press, 1977.

Jakobson, Roman. *Coup d'oeil sur le développement de la sémiotique*. Bloomington: Research Center for Language and Semiotic Studies, Indiana University, 1971.

Kowzan, Tadeusz, ed. *Analyse sémiologique du spectacle théâtral*. Lyon: Centre d'Etudes et de Recherches Théâtrales, Université de Lyon, II, 1976.

———. *Littérature et spectacle*. The Hague: Mouton, 1975.

Kristeva, Julia. *Sémiotikè: Recherches pour une sémanalyse*. Paris: Seuil, 1968.

Langer, Suzanne K. *Feeling and Form*. New York: Scribner's, 1953.

Lotman, Yuri M. *Analysis of the Poetic Text*. Trans. D. Barton Johnson. Ann Arbor, Mich.: Ardis, 1976.

Macksey, Richard, and Eugenio Donato. *The Structuralist Controversy: The Languages of Criticism and the Sciences of Man*. Baltimore: Johns Hopkins University Press, 1970.

Matejka, Ladislaw, and Irwin R. Titunik, eds. *Semiotics of Art: Prague School Contributions*. Cambridge, Mass.: MIT Press, 1976.

Modern Drama 25, i (1982): 1–81. Special issue on Theory of Drama and Performance.

Morris, Charles. *Foundations of a Theory of Signs*. Foundations of The Unity of Science, Vol. 1, No. 2. Chicago: University of Chicago Press, 1938.

———. *Signification and Significance*. Cambridge, Mass.: MIT Press, 1964.

Mounin, Georges. *Introduction à la sémiologie*. Paris: Les Editions de Minuit, 1969.

Norris, Christopher. *Deconstruction: Theory and Practice*. London and New York: Methuen, 1982.

Organon 80 (1980). Special issue on "Sémiologie et théâtre."

Pavis, Patrice. *Dictionnaire du théâtre*. Paris: Editions sociales, 1980.

———. *Languages of the Stage: Essays in the Semiotics of Theatre*. New York: PAJ Publications, 1982.

———. *Problèmes de sémiologie théâtrale*. Québec: Les Presses de l'Université Québec, 1976.

Peirce, Charles S. *Collected Papers*. 8 vols. Cambridge, Mass.: Harvard University Press, 1931–58.

Poetics 6 (1977) and 13 (1984). Special issues on "The Formal Study of Drama." Ed. Solomon Marcus.

Poetics Today 2, no. 3 (Spring 1981): 1–270. Issue devoted to drama, theater, and performance from a semiotic perspective.

Pratt, Mary Louise. *Toward a Speech Act Theory of Literary Discourse.* Bloomington: Indiana University Press, 1977.

Saussure, Ferdinand de. *Course in General Linguistics.* Trans. Wade Baskin. New York: McGraw-Hill, 1966.

Savona, Jeanette, ed. *Théâtre et théâtralité: Actes du Colloque 'Théâtralité,'* Toronto, 1980. Montréal: Editions littéraires, 1981.

Schechner, Richard. *The End of Humanism.* New York: Performing Arts Journal Publications, 1982.

―――. *Public Domain.* Indianapolis: Bobbs-Merrill, 1969.

Searle, John R. *Speech Acts: An Essay in the Philosophy of Language.* Cambridge: Cambridge University Press, 1969.

Sebeok, Thomas A., Alfred S. Hayes, and Mary C. Bateson, eds. *Approaches to Semiotics.* The Hague: Mouton, 1964.

―――, *The Sign and Its Masters.* Austin: University of Texas Press, 1979.

―――, ed. *Style in Language.* New York: Wiley, 1960.

―――, ed. *The Tell-Tale Sign.* Lisse: Peter de Ridder, 1975.

Semiotext(e) 3, no. 1 (1978). Special issue on Nietzsche.

Sub-stance 18/19 (1977). Special issue on "Theater in France: Ten Years of Research."

Ubersfeld, Anne. *L'Ecole du spectateur.* Paris: Editions sociales, 1981.

―――. *Lire le théâtre.* Paris: Editions sociales, 1977.

Veltrusky, Jiri. *Drama as Literature.* Lisse: Peter de Ridder, 1977.

Articles and Essays

Alter, Jean. "Coding Dramatic Efficiency in Plays: From Text to Stage." *Semiotics* 28, no. 3/4 (1979): 247–57.

―――. "From Text to Performance: Semiotics of Theatrality." *Poetics Today* 2, no. 3 (Spring 1981): 113–39.

―――. "Vers de mathématexte au théâtre: en codant Godot." In *Sémiologie de la représentation.* Ed. André Helbo, 42–61. Brussels: Complexe, 1975.

Amossy, Ruth. "Semiology and Theater: By Way of Introduction." *Poetics Today* 2, no. 3 (Spring 1981): 5–10.

―――. "Toward a Rhetoric of the Stage: The Scenic Realization of Verbal Clichés." *Poetics Today* 2, no. 3 (Spring 1981): 49–63.

Avigal, Shoshana, and Schlomith Rimmon-Kenan. "What Do Brook's Bricks Mean? Toward a Theory of the 'Mobility' of Objects in Theatrical Discourse." *Poetics Today* 2, no. 3 (Spring 1981): 11–34.

Barker, Donald. "A Structural Theory of Theatre." *Yale/Theatre* 8, no. 1 (1976): 55–61.

Barthes, Roland. "Barthes on Theatre." *Theatre Quarterly* 33 (1979): 25–30.

―――. "Literature and Signification." In *Critical Essays.* Trans. Richard Howard, 261–67. Evanston: Northwestern University Press, 1972.

Basnett-McGuire, Susan. "An Introduction to Theatre Semiotics." *Theatre Quarterly* 38 (1980): 47–53.

Bateson, Gregory. "A Theory of Play and Fantasy." In *Steps to an Ecology of Mind,* 150–66. London: Granada Publishing, 1973.

Blau, Herbert. "Letting Be Be Finale of Seem: The Future of an Illusion." In *Performance in Postmodern Culture.* Ed. Michel Benamou and Charles Caramello, 59–77. Madison, Wis.: Coda Press, 1977.

Bogatyrev, Petr. "Forms and Functions of Folk Theatre." Trans. Bruce Kochis. In *Semiotics of Art: Prague School Contributions.* Ed. Ladislaw Matejka and Irwin R. Titunik, 51–56. Cambridge: MIT Press, 1976.

_____. "Semiotics in the Folk Theatre." Trans. Bruce Kochis. In *Semiotics of Art: Prague School Contributions.* Ed. Ladislaw Matejka and Irwin R. Titunik, 33–49. Cambridge: MIT Press, 1976.

Brusak, Karel. "Signs in the Chinese Theater." Trans. Karel Brusak. In *Semiotics of Art: Prague School Contributions.* Ed. Ladislaw Matejka and Irwin R. Titunik, 59–73. Cambridge: MIT Press, 1976.

Campeanu, Pavel. "Un rôle secondaire: le spectateur." In *Sémiologie de la représentation.* Ed. André Helbo, 96–111. Brussels: Complexe, 1975.

Coppieters, Frank. "Performance and Perception." *Poetics Today* 2, no. 3 (Spring 1981): 35–48.

Corvin, Michel. "Approche sémiologique d'un texte dramatique: *La Parodie* de A. Adamov." *Littérature* 9 (1973): 86–100.

_____. "A propos des spectacles de R. Wilson: Essai de lecture sémiologique." *Cahiers Renaud-Barrault* 77 (1971): 90–111.

Durand, Régis. "Problèmes de l'analyse structurale et sémiotique de la forme théâtrale." In *Sémiologie de la représentation.* Ed. André Helbo, 112–21. Brussels: Complexe, 1975.

Eco, Umberto. "Semiotics of Theatrical Performance." *The Drama Review* 21 (1977): 107–17.

Elam, Keir. "Language in the Theater." *Sub-stance* 18/19 (1977): 139–61.

Féral, Josette. "For a Semiotics of the Theater." Trans. Karen Woodward. *Sub-stance* 18/19 (1977): 135–38.

Handke, Peter. "Nauseated by Language." Interview with Artur Joseph. Trans. E.B. Ashton. *The Drama Review* 15 (1970): 56–61.

Hannaford, Stephen. "Symbols, Emblems, Tokens." *Theatre Journal* 33 (1981): 467–76.

Helbo, André. "Le code théâtral." In *Sémiologie de la représentation.* Ed. André Helbo, 12–27. Brussels: Complexe, 1975.

_____. "Pour un proprium de la représentation théâtrale." In *Sémiologie de la représentation.* Ed. André Helbo, 62–72. Brussels: Complexe, 1975.

_____. "La représentation dans le récit." In *Sémiologie de la représentation.* Ed. André Helbo, 28–32. Brussels: Complexe, 1975.

_____. "The Semiology of the Theater, or: Communication Swamped." *Poetics Today* 2, no. 3 (Spring 1981): 105–11.

_____. "Theater as Representation." Trans. Rose M. Avila and Roland A. Champagne. *Sub-stance* 18/19 (1977): 56–61.

Honzl, Jindrich. "Dynamics of the Sign in the Theater." Trans. I.R. Titunik. In *Semiotics of Art: Prague School Contributions.* Ed. Ladislaw Matejka and Irwin R. Titunik, 74–93. Cambridge: MIT Press, 1976.

_____. "The Hierarchy of Dramatic Devices." Trans. Susan Larson. In *Semiotics of Art: Prague School Contributions.* Ed. Ladislaw Matejka and Irwin R. Titunik, 118–27. Cambridge, Mass: MIT Press, 1976.

Issacharoff, Michael. "Space and Reference in Drama." *Poetics Today* 2, no. 3 (Spring 1981): 211–24.

Kaisergruber, Danielle. "Reading and Producing Theater." Trans. Carl R. Lovitt and Roland A. Champagne. *Sub-stance,* 18/19 (1977): 163–71.

Kowzan, Tadeusz. "Signe zéro de la parole." *Degrés* 31 (1982): 1–16.

_____. "The Sign in the Theatre." Trans. Simon Pleasance. *Diogenes* 61 (1968): 52–80.

_____. "Le Texte et son interprétation théâtrale." *Semiotica* 33 (1981): 201–10.

Kristeva, Julia. "Modern Theater Does Not Take (a) Place." *Sub-stance* 18/19 (1977): 131–34.

Krysinski, Wladimir. "Semiotic Modalities of the Body in Modern Theater." Trans. Raili Mikkanen. *Poetics Today* 2, no. 3 (Spring 1981): 141–61.

Marcus, Solomon. "Stratégie des personnages dramatiques." In *Sémiologie de la représentation.* Ed. André Helbo, 73–95. Brussels: Complexe, 1975.

Mukarovsky, Jan. "Art as Semiotic Fact." Trans. I.R. Titunik. In *Semiotics of Art: Prague School Contributions.* Ed. Ladislaw Matejka and Irwin R. Titunik, 3–9. Cambridge, Mass: MIT Press, 1976.

Palmer, Richard. "Toward a Postmodern Hermeneutics of Performance." In *Performance in Postmodern Culture.* Ed. Michel Benamou and Charles Caramello, 19–32. Madison, Wis.: Coda Press, 1977.

Passow, Wilfried. "The Analysis of Theatrical Performance." Trans. R. Strauss. *Poetics Today* 2, no. 3 (Spring 1981): 237–54.

Pavis, Patrice. "The Interplay between Avant-Garde Theatre and Semiology." Trans. Jill Daugherty. *Performing Arts Journal* 15 (Vol. 5, No. 3) (1981): 75–86.

————. "Problems of a Semiology of Theatrical Gesture." Trans. Elena Biller-Lappin. *Poetics Today* 2, no. 3 (Spring 1981): 65–93.

————. "Production et réception au théâtre: la concrétisation du texte dramatique et spectaculaire." *Revue de sciences humaines* 60 (1983): 51–88.

Rabkin, Gerald. "The Play of Misreading: text/theatre/deconstruction." *Performing Arts Journal* 19 (1983): 44–60.

Revzina, O.G., and Revsin, I.I. "Experimentation sémiotique chez E. Ionesco (*La Cantatrice chauve* et *La Leçon*)." *Semiotica* 4, no. 3 (1971): 240–62.

————. "A Semiotic Experiment on Stage: The Violation of the Postulate of Normal Communication as a Dramatic Device." *Semiotica* 14, no. 3 (1975): 245–68.

Rothenberg, Jerome. "New Models, New Visions: Some Notes Toward a Poetics of Performance." In *Performance in Postmodern Culture.* Ed. Michel Benamou and Charles Caramello, 11–17. Madison, Wis.: Coda Press, 1977.

Sacksteder, William. "Elements of the Dramatic Model." *Diogenes* 52 (1975): 26–54.

Schaeffer, Pierre. "Représentation et communication." In *Sémiologie de la représentation.* Ed. André Helbo, 167–93. Brussels: Complexe, 1975.

Schechner, Richard. "Drama, Script, Theatre, and Performance.' *The Drama Review* 17 (1973): 5–36.

Segre, Cesare. "Narratology and Theater." Trans. John Meddemmen. *Poetics Today* 2, no. 3 (Spring 1981): 95–104.

Serpieri, Alessandro, et al. "Toward a Segmentation of the Dramatic Text." *Poetics Today* 2, no. 3 (Spring 1981): 163–200.

Turner, Victor. "Frame, Flow and Reflection: Ritual and Drama as Public Liminality." In *Performance in Postmodern Culture.* Ed. Michel Benamou and Charles Caramello, 33–55. Madison, Wis.: Coda Press, 1977.

Ubersfeld, Anne. "Adamov Today: A Reconsideration of Planchon's A.A." Trans. Michel Grimaud. *Sub-stance* 18/19 (1977): 182–88.

————. "Notes sur la dénégation théâtrale." In *La Relation théâtrale.* Ed. V. Bourgy and R. Durand, 11–25. Lille: Presses de l'Université de Lille, 1980.

————. "The Space of *Phèdre*." Trans. Mya Weinberger. *Poetics Today* 2, no. 3 (Spring 1981): 201–10.

Veinstein, André. "Teaching Theater in the French University: Questions from one who is expected to give answers." Trans. Roxanne Hannay. *Sub-stance* 18/19 (1977): 189–92.

Veltrusky, Jiri. "Construction of Semantic Components." In *Semiotics of Art: Prague School Contributions.* Ed. Ladislaw Matejka and Irwin R. Titunik, 134–44. Cambridge, Mass.: MIT Press, 1976.

————. "Dramatic Text as a Component of Theater." In *Semiotics of Art: Prague School Contributions.* Ed. Ladislaw Matejka and Irwin R. Titunik, 94–117. Cambridge, Mass.: MIT Press, 1976.

————. "The Prague School Theory of Theater." *Poetics Today* 2, no. 3 (Spring 1981): 225–35.

Index